Social Perspectives in the 21st Century

Life Course and Society

SOCIAL PERSPECTIVES IN THE 21ST CENTURY

JASON L. POWELL - SERIES AUTHOR –
THE UNIVERSITY OF CHESTER, U.K.

Life Course and Society
Jason L. Powell
2018. ISBN: 978-1-53613-848-1

The Power of Global Aging
Jason L. Powell
2018. ISBN: 978-1-53613-846-7

Feminist Social Theory
Jason L. Powell
2014. ISBN: 978-1-62948-535-5

**Aging, Culture and Society:
A Sociological Approach**
Jason L. Powell
2013. ISBN: 978-1-62808-960-8

Power and Aging: A Macro and Micro Analysis
Jason L. Powell
2014. ISBN: 978-1-62948-534-8

Aging, Risk and Globalization
Jason L. Powell
2013. ISBN: 978-1-62808-902-8

**Theorizing Community Care:
From Disciplinary Power to Governmentality to Personal Care**
Jason L. Powell
2014. ISBN: 978-1-62948-532-4

Contemporary Issues in Modern Society
Jason L. Powell
2013. ISBN: 978-1-62808-212-8

The "Management of Aging" and the Dark Side of Modernity
Jason L. Powell
2014. ISBN: 978-1-62948-533-1

**Education, Employment and Pensions:
A Critical Narrative**
Jason L. Powell
2013. ISBN: 978-1-62808-383-5

From Historical Social Theory to Foucault
Jason L. Powell
2013. ISBN: 978-1-62618-345-2

Global Aging, China and Urbanization
Jason L. Powell
2013. ISBN: 978-1-62808-452-8

Helping Professions and Aging: Theory, Policy and Practice
Jason L. Powell
2013. ISBN: 978-1-62808-381-1

Issues in Crime, Criminal Justice and Aging
Jason L. Powell
2013. ISBN: 978-1-62808-890-8

Issues in Sociology
Jason L. Powell
2013. ISBN: 978-1-62808-211-1

Key Thinkers in Social Science
Jason L. Powell
2013. ISBN: 978-1-62808-453-5

Neo-Liberalism and the Power of Globalization
Jason L. Powell
2013. ISBN: 978-1-62948-469-3

Rethinking Social Welfare
Jason L. Powell
2013. ISBN: 978-1-62808-330-9

Social Philosophy, Age and Aging
Jason L. Powell
2013. ISBN: 978-1-62808-382-8

Social Work, Performativity and Personalization
Jason L. Powell
2013. ISBN: 978-1-62808-903-5

Symbolic Interactionism
Jason L. Powell
2013. ISBN: 978-1-62808-213-5

The Aging Body
Jason L. Powell
2013. ISBN: 978-1-62808-380-4

The Social Analysis of Emotion and Trust
Jason L. Powell
2013. ISBN: 978-1-62948-120-3

Understanding Foucault: For Beginners
Jason L. Powell
2013. ISBN: 978-1-62417-195-6

Understanding Power and Emotion: An Introduction
Jason L. Powell
2013. ISBN: 978-1-62417-200-7

Understanding Risk and Trust: A Short Conceptual Examination
Jason L. Powell
2013. ISBN: 978-1-62417-202-1

Baudrillard and Postmodernism
Jason L. Powell
2012. ISBN: 978-1-62257-541-1

Feminism
Jason L. Powell
2012. ISBN: 978-1-62257-540-4

Foucault: Issues and Legacy
Jason L. Powell
2012. ISBN: 978-1-62257-539-8

Habermas
Jason L. Powell
2012. ISBN: 978-1-62257-542-8

SOCIAL PERSPECTIVES IN THE 21ST CENTURY

LIFE COURSE AND SOCIETY

JASON L. POWELL

nova science publishers
New York

Copyright © 2018 by Nova Science Publishers, Inc.

All rights reserved. No part of this book may be reproduced, stored in a retrieval system or transmitted in any form or by any means: electronic, electrostatic, magnetic, tape, mechanical photocopying, recording or otherwise without the written permission of the Publisher.

We have partnered with Copyright Clearance Center to make it easy for you to obtain permissions to reuse content from this publication. Simply navigate to this publication's page on Nova's website and locate the "Get Permission" button below the title description. This button is linked directly to the title's permission page on copyright.com. Alternatively, you can visit copyright.com and search by title, ISBN, or ISSN.

For further questions about using the service on copyright.com, please contact:
Copyright Clearance Center
Phone: +1-(978) 750-8400   Fax: +1-(978) 750-4470   E-mail: info@copyright.com.

NOTICE TO THE READER

The Publisher has taken reasonable care in the preparation of this book, but makes no expressed or implied warranty of any kind and assumes no responsibility for any errors or omissions. No liability is assumed for incidental or consequential damages in connection with or arising out of information contained in this book. The Publisher shall not be liable for any special, consequential, or exemplary damages resulting, in whole or in part, from the readers' use of, or reliance upon, this material. Any parts of this book based on government reports are so indicated and copyright is claimed for those parts to the extent applicable to compilations of such works.

Independent verification should be sought for any data, advice or recommendations contained in this book. In addition, no responsibility is assumed by the publisher for any injury and/or damage to persons or property arising from any methods, products, instructions, ideas or otherwise contained in this publication.

This publication is designed to provide accurate and authoritative information with regard to the subject matter covered herein. It is sold with the clear understanding that the Publisher is not engaged in rendering legal or any other professional services. If legal or any other expert assistance is required, the services of a competent person should be sought. FROM A DECLARATION OF PARTICIPANTS JOINTLY ADOPTED BY A COMMITTEE OF THE AMERICAN BAR ASSOCIATION AND A COMMITTEE OF PUBLISHERS.

Additional color graphics may be available in the e-book version of this book.

Library of Congress Cataloging-in-Publication Data

ISBN: 978-1-53613-848-1

Published by Nova Science Publishers, Inc. † New York

CONTENTS

Chapter 1	Introduction: The Dominance of Biomedicine and Colonisisation of Life Course	1
Chapter 2	The Global Context of Aging	9
Chapter 3	Age, Professional Power and Social Policy in the United Kingdom	23
Chapter 4	Aging, Foucault and the Life Course	45
Chapter 5	Trust, the Life Course and Social Relations	67
Conclusion		99
References		101
Author's Contact Information		115
Index		117

Chapter 1

INTRODUCTION: THE DOMINANCE OF BIOMEDICINE AND COLONISISATION OF LIFE COURSE

This book explores the concept of the life course and its relationship to society. As part of this process, 'gerontology' is a broad discipline which encompasses psychological, biological and social analyses of aging (Longino and Powell, 2004). Since the beginning of the twentieth century, the 'bio-medical' study of aging consisting of biological and psychological explanatory frameworks has dominated the disciplinary development of gerontology. There are important implications here for how aging is viewed not just by bio-medical models of aging but for how society and its arrangement of political and economic structures create and sanction social policies grounded in such knowledge bases (cf. Powell, 2001). Since the beginning of the 21st century, there has also been a new emergence of anti-aging movement led by Aubrey De Grey which has startling continuities with traditional bio-gerontology – aging is seen as a disease.

Such knowledge bases are focused on: one, 'aging' as a disease refers to the internal and external physiological deficits that take place in the individual body; two, 'psychological aging' is understood as the decline in mental functioning – emotional and cognitive capacities. Anti-aging can be distinguished from social construction of aging: one, focusing on the bio-psychological constituent of aging; two, on how aging has been socially constructed. One perspective is driven from 'within' and privileges the expression from inner to outer worlds. The other is much more concerned with the power of external structures that shape individuals experiences and their bodies.

Estes and Binney (1989) have used the expression 'biomedicalization of aging' which has two closely related narratives: one, the *social construction of aging* as a medical problem; two, *ageist practices and policies growing out of thinking of aging* as a medical problem. They suggest:

> '*Equating old age with illness has encouraged society to think about aging as pathological or abnormal.* The undesirability of conditions labelled as sickness or illness transfer to those who have these conditions, shaping the attitudes of the persons themselves and those of others towards them. Sick role expectations may result in such behaviors as social withdrawal, reduction in activity, increased dependency and the loss of effectiveness and personal control – all of which may result in the social control of the elderly through medical definition, management and treatment'. (Estes and Binney, 1989, 588) (*my emphasis*)

Estes and Binney (1989) highlight how individual lives and physical and mental capacities which were thought to be determined solely by biological and psychological factors, are, in fact, heavily influenced by *social environments* in which people live – yet bio-medicine is a powerful domain.

Bio-gerontology is a fundamental domain where medical discourses on anti-aging have become located and this is very powerful in articulating 'truths' about anti-aging (Estes and Binney, 1989). Similarly, biomedical models of aging have also been prone to what Harry R. Moody (1998) refers to as an "amalgam of advocacy and science" in a neo-liberal attempt to position individualized perceptions of aging. Under the guise of science and its perceived tenets of value-freedom, objectivity and precision (Biggs, 1993), bio-medical gerontology has a cloth of legitimacy. However, Powell and Phillipson (2004) ask a fundamental question: how has bio-gerontology not only stabilized itself with a positivist discourse that not reflects history but also the total preoccupation of science and the 'problems' of aging?

In addition, bio-gerontology represents the contested terrain of decisions reflecting both normative claims and technological possibilities. Bio-gerontology refers to medical techniques that privilege a biological and psychological understanding of the human condition and rely upon 'scientific assumptions' that position attitudes to aging in society for their existence and practice (Powell and Biggs, 2000). As Arthur Frank (1991, 6) notes, the bio-medical model occupies a privileged position in contemporary culture and society:

'Bio-Medicine [occupies] a paramount place among those institutions and practices by which the body is conceptualized, represented and responded to. At present our capacity to experience the body directly, or theorize it indirectly, is inextricably medicalized not sociologized'.

So scientific medicine is based on bio-gerontology. Some doctrines of the biomedical model more closely reflect the basic sciences while others refer to the primary concern of medicine, namely diseases located in the human body. Most important is that these beliefs hold together, thereby reinforcing one another and forming a coherent orientation toward the mind and body. Indeed, the mind-body dualism had become the location of regimen and control for emergence of scientific in positivist methodological search for objective 'truth' (Longino and Powell, 2004). The end product of this process in western society is the "bio-medical model". Some doctrines of the biomedical model more closely reflect the basic sciences while others refer to the primary concern of medicine, namely diseases located in the human body. Most important is that these beliefs hold together, thereby reinforcing one another and forming a coherent whole (Longino and Powell, 2004). By developing an all-encompassing range of bio-medical discourses, many forms of social injustice could be justified as 'natural', inevitable and necessary for the successful equilibrium of the social whole such as mandatory retirement and allocation of pensions (Powell and Phillipson, 2004).

THE BIO-MEDICAL MODEL: BIOLOGICAL AND PSYCHOLOGICAL AGING – SCIENCE OF AGING?

There has long been a tendency in matters of aging and old age to reduce the social experience of aging to its biological dimension from which are derived a set of normative 'stages' which over-determine the experience of aging. Accordingly being 'old', for example, would primarily be an individualized experience of adaptation to inevitable physical and mental decline and of preparation for death (Powell, 2000). The paradox of course is that the homogenising of the experience of old age which the reliance on the biological dimension of old age entails is in fact one of the key elements of the dominant discourse on aging and old age.

Biological approaches to aging have focused on searching for the reasons why and how human beings change over time in terms of physical and physiological characteristics. Bromley (1988, 77) suggests that aging is a degenerative process and contends that:

> '... aging can be conveniently defined as a complex, cumulative, time related process of biological and psychological deterioration occupying the post-development phase of life.'

Furthermore, according to Alessio (1999) the 'passage of time' for human organisms are related to physical changes in and on the body: 'hair loss' or 'graying of hair', 'decrease in reproductive system', and 'cardiovascular functioning' are examples. These processes have been called 'physiological changes' that are designed to contribute to the body's ability to function as it traverses across the aging process.

Such bodily processes are designed to maintain a balance of internal working conditions coined *homeostasis* (Morgan and Kunkel, 1999). A key example of this scientific assumption is the relationship of oxygen to blood system. Oxygen is transported by hemoglobin in the blood system to the body's 100 trillion cells (Morgan and Kunkel, 1999). According to Alessio (1999) the inability of the body to maintain homeostasis compromises 'normal functions' and 'survival'. The key issue here is one of internal body and functions; however, there is another wider questions whether changes to the body exemplify 'decline'.

Kunkel and Morgan (1999) suggest that aging is often associated with a reduced ability to maintain homeostasis. According to Crook (1995) the potential of oxygen to all body cells decreases with age. However, changes outside the body may also disturb homeostasis such as environmental pollution (Phillipson, 1998). Although, the dominant narrative in the biological explanation of aging is that the ability to perform bodily functions will affect an individuals survival. The causal factors of the breakdown of these functions are essentially contested. Major causes of death at the turn of the twentieth century were infections and diseases, whereas major deaths in western societies at turn of 21st century are chronic diseases: cardio-vascular disease, cancer and stroke (Tinker, 1997). A posing question is whether these changes to the body are inevitable and natural consequences of aging? Aging it seems is linked with increased 'risk' of illness and disease (Biggs, 1993). The relationship is not necessarily causal: aging does not cause disease and disease does not cause aging.

According to Timiras (1997) biological aging affects every individual, evidencing itself overtly and covertly at different ages and in different organs and systems depending on a whole series of cascading effects (Timiras, 1997). Secondly, Timiras (1997) sees aging as a 'deleterious' process, involving the functioning of cells and therefore organs and the organism itself.

'We also know that age-related changes that do occur have a limiting effect on a number of bodily functions… a reduction in the accuracy of maintaining posture increases the amount of sway in the standing positions' (Timiras, 1997, 53).

Another prominent example of biological aging is a focus on the pathological formation of 'impairment in the body' (Bromley, 1988). It is partly assumed to be due to the aging process but it may be made worse by the 'dementing process' such as Alzheimer's Disease (Crook, 1995). According to Crook (1995) 'postural hypotension' is another of those problems that are age-related. In age-related vulnerabilities physiological systems decline with age resulting in a shift in the accuracy of the body to control the chemical and cellular environment and thus leaving individuals more prone to diseases of aging. In other words, the biological facet of aging is related to internal problems of the body as a person grows older. Coupled with this, there are certain biological viewpoints that suggest that older people have many 'inevitable medical problems':

> 'In fact, if one were to look at the presenting medical problems of the elderly, six symptoms would stand out: mental confusion, respiratory problems, incontinence, postural instability and falls, immobility and social breakdown'. (Timiras, 1997, 54)

For Allesio (1999) such an approach has suggested the following theoretical assumptions: that the human body is portrayed as a machine and overworked machines and human bodies 'wear out' and 'decline'; the human body grows but 'decays' with time; 'abnormal cells' are formed as a result or damage to DNA from 'internal problems', all future cells are marked to be different, 'in error' and 'inferior' to the original intact parent cell; human skin 'wrinkles' over time with passing of pigment cells; Aging and death are built in programmed events that result from genes 'turning on' and 'turning off' – for example, Allesio suggests there is gendered evidence for this amongst females such as menopause events; bodily aging causes problems of vision, hearing and sensory function and balance. Healthy living and diet are seen as key shields to curtail the problems of biological 'aging'. The individualized notion of aging as espoused by biological aging suggests that the body is in decline but as an individual ages especially venal in 'old age'. The term terminal decline or terminal drop has been defined by Riegel and Riegel (1972, 366) as 'a sudden drop in performance occurring within 5 years prior to death'. As a phenomena, terminal decline has been observed by many researchers including Jarvik and Falek (1963) that relate the terminal drop to the area of intellectual functioning in old age (Jarvik and Falek, 1963).

An interesting question is whether these physical changes are inevitable consequences of aging? The perceptions of aging through biology not only has postulated perspectives about aging but also there has been the psychological approach that has helped to coalesce particular discourses about aging.

Biological characteristics associated with aging have been used to construct scientific representations of aging in modern society. The characteristics of biological aging as associated with loss of skin elasticity, wrinkled skin, hair loss or physical frailty perpetuates powerful assumptions that help facilitate attitudes and perceptions of aging. It may be argued that rather than provide a scientific explanation of aging, such an approach homogenizes the experiences of aging by suggesting these characteristics are universal, natural and inevitable. These assumptions are powerful in creating a knowledge base for health and social welfare professionals who work with older people in particular medical settings such as a hospital or general doctors surgery and also for social workers (Powell and Biggs, 2004).

THE DARK SIDE OF BIO-MEDICAL ASSUMPTIONS

Biggs (1993) suggests that a prevailing ideology of ageism manifests by bio-gerontology by its suggestion that persons with traits have entered a spiral of decay, decline and deterioriation. Along with this goes certain assumptions about the ways in which people with outward signs of aging are likely to think and behave. For example, there are assumptions that 'older people are poor drivers' or that older people have little interest in relationships that involve sexual pleasure that are all explained away by 'decline' and 'deteriorition' master narratives that comprise an aging culture. The effects of the 'decline' and 'decay' analogies can be most clearly seen in the dominance of medico-technical solutions to the problems that aging and even an 'aging population' (Phillipson, 1998) is thought to pose. Here, the bio-medical model has both come to colonise notions of age and reinforce ageist social prejudices to the extent that 'decline' has come to stand for the process of aging itself (Powell, 1999).

Conclusion

Biggs and Powell (2001) argue that people themselves derive their sense of identity in later life from the achievements of the past and what remains to be accomplished in the future, rather than from a set of stereotypical—usually negative bio-biological—attributes of old age. Bio-medical scholars can study persons of a certain age, but their reality seldom reflects that of the subjects of study when understanding human aging is ignored because becoming, and being, old are embodied and experiential social processes not bio-medical processes of 'terminal drop'.

The re-territorialisation of a *social* understanding of the life course in society, is a strategy that parallels the denial of older people's sense of agency and subjectivity within the main traditions of the bio-medical model. From our discussion, it would seem that aging is a mode of embodied subjectivity for social gerontologists to unravel.

Chapter 2

THE GLOBAL CONTEXT OF AGING

INTRODUCTION

In the latter half of the last century, the world's developed nations completed a long process of demographic transition (Phillipson, 1998). We can see demographic transition as a shift from a period of high mortality, short lives, and large families to one with a longer life expectancy for an aging population and far fewer children (Powell, 2005). This transformation has taken many years across the globe but particularly in Europe and North America as small unit families moved from agrarian mode of production to urban cities; basic public health measures steadily reduced the risk of contagious disease; and modern medicine has prolonged lives to unprecedented lengths (Giddens, 1993). In developing countries, this demographic transition is certainly underway, though these countries vary widely at their places along the spectrum. Low birth rates and the resultant population decrease have received considerable media attention, particularly in Europe and parts of eastern Asia (Bengston and Lowenstein 2004). Historically, when demographers projected national and global populations, the projections commonly assumed that birth rates would decline globally but only to the "two-child" family, i.e., two children per woman or per couple on average (Phillipson, 1998). An assumption that fertility would fall below this rate would have some consequences: a decrease in population size and an aging population who would depend upon a dwindling number of younger workers. Today, the global population has come to what we may call a great "demographic divide". Very low birth rates have inflicted long-lasting alterations upon the age structure of populational aging (Phillipson, 1998).

In order to examine such complex and vast demographic changes, academic researchers use a variety of methodological tools to find, collate and interpret such changes. The forecasted rise in the number of older people aged 75+ over the next 20 years will lead to an expansion of demand for health care services, housing accommodation and pensions for aging populations. Direct statistical data about aging populations come from vital statistics registries that track all births and deaths as well as certain changes in legal status such as marriage, divorce, and migration (registration of place of residence) (Phillipson 1998). In developed countries with good registration systems (such as the United States and much of Europe), registry statistics are the best method for measuring the number of births and deaths in populations (Bengtson and Lowenstein 2004). A Census is also usually conducted by a national government and attempts to enumerate every person in a country (Gavrilov and Gavrilova 1991). However, in contrast to vital statistics data, which are typically collected continuously and summarized on an annual basis, the American Community Surveys typically occur only every 10 years (Phillipson 1998). Analyses are conducted after a Census to estimate how much over or undercounting took place. Censuses collect information about families or households, as well as about such individual characteristics as age, sex, marital status, literacy/education, employment status and occupation, and geographical location (Giddens 1993). They may also collect data on migration (or place of birth or of previous residence), language, religion, nationality (or ethnicity or race), and citizenship. In nation states in which the vital registration system may be incomplete, Censuses are also used as a direct source of information about fertility and mortality; for example the censuses of the People's Republic of China gather information on births and deaths that occurred in the 18 months immediately preceding the census (Cook and Powell, 2007). This is a point that will be picked up later.

GLOBAL AGING

We can usually consider various dimensions to measure global aging such as demographic, socio-economic, health, intergenerational support, activities in later life, social security, dependency rates and human right issues (Phillipson 1998). The datasets or statistics that are used to measure the global aging are basically demographically and medically oriented. For example, *low birthrates, life expectancy and dependency rates.* While the proportions of older people in a population are typically highest in more developed countries because of measurement data of *low birth rates* and high *life expectancies* which are used to understand global aging, the most rapid increases in older populations are actually occurring in the less developed world (Cook and Powell, 2007). Between 2006 and 2030, the increasing number of older people in less developed countries is projected to escalate by 140% as compared to an increase of 51% in more developed countries (Krug, 2002). A key feature of population aging is the progressive aging of the older population itself. Demographers contrast the "old" (65+) with the "oldest old" (85+) and that the oldest old population is growing at an even more rapid pace than the overall old population. Over time, more older people survive to even more advanced ages. Around the world, the 85-and-over population is projected to increase 151% between 2005 and 2030, compared to a 104% increase for the population age 65 and over and a 21% increase for the population under age 65 (Bengtson and Lowenstein 2004). The most striking increase will occur in Japan: by 2030, nearly 24% of all older Japanese are expected to be at least 85 years old (Kim and Lee 2007). As life expectancy increases and people aged 85 and over increase in number, four-generation families may become more common. *Dependency rates*, that is the number of dependants related to those of working age have altered little over the twentieth and twenty first centuries. The reason there has been so little change during a period of so-called rapid aging populations is that there has been a fall in the total fertility rate (the average number of children that would be born to each woman if the current age-specific birth rates persisted throughout her child-bearing life).

In every society in the world, there is concern about population aging and its consequences for nation states, for sovereign governments and for individuals. The global population is aging. Aging itself is a triumph of our times – a product of improved public health, sanitation and development. Yet over 100 million older people live on less than a dollar a day. In 1950, 8 out of every 100 people were over 60. By 2050, 22 out of every 100 people will be over 60. By 2045, the global population of people aged 60 years and over will likely surpass, for the first time in history, the number of children under age 15 (Powell, 2005). The increasing share of older people in the world's population results from a combination of hugely increased life expectancy and reduced fertility. Total fertility is expected to decline from 2.82 children per woman in 1995-2000 to 2.15 children per woman in 2045-2050. Life expectancy worldwide is expected to increase by 11 years, from 65 in 1995-2000 to 76 in 2045-2050, despite the impact of HIV/AIDS (Phillipson 1998). Most of the world's older people live in developing countries (Krug, 2002). Even in the poorest countries, life expectancy is increasing and the number of older people is growing. In 2000, there were 374 million people over 60 in developing countries – 62% of the world's older people. In 2015, there will be 597 million older people in developing countries – 67% of the world's older people (Bengston and Lowenstein 2004). In 2005, one in twelve people in developing countries are over 60. By 2015, one in ten people in developing countries will be over 60 and, by 2050, one in five people in developing countries will be over 60. In every region, the rate of population increase for the 65-and-over age group is higher than for the under-14 age group and the 15-64 age group (Bengston and Lowenstein 2004).

There are more older women and they are more likely to be poor. The majority of older persons globally are women. In 2006, there are 82 men for every 100 women over 60 worldwide (Powell, 2005). In developing countries, the gap is less wide: there are 85 men for every 100 women over

60. However, with age this gap increases – for over 80s, there are only 73 men for every 100.

In order to see how it plays out in the Americas, Europe and Africa does illustrate some key differences and issues on populational growth.

AMERICAS

Since the turn of the 20th century, the life expectancy of people born in North America (including Mexico) has increased by approximately 25 years and the proportion of persons 65 years or older has increased from 4% to over 13% (Estes 2001). By the year 2030, one in five individuals in the U.S. is expected to be 65 years or older and people age 85 and older make up the fastest growing segment of the population. In 2000, there were 34 million people aged 65 or older in the United States that represented 13% of the overall population (Estes 2001). By 2030 there will be 70 million over 65 in the United States, more than twice their number in 2000. Longino (1994) believes that thanks to better health, changing living arrangements and improved assistive devices, the future may not be as negative as we think when we consider an aging population (1994). 31 million people, or 12 percent of the total population, are aged 65 and older. In another 35 years, the older adult population should double again. The aging population is not only growing rapidly, but it is also getting older, as evidenced by the average age of the population:

Although the proportion of the oldest old is expected to increase by 2045, in many countries, including the US, the proportion will likely remain stable until 2030. In the United States, the oldest old accounted for 14% of all older people in 2005. By 2030, this percentage is unlikely to change because the aging baby boom generation will continue to enter the ranks of the 65-and-over population (Bengtson and Lowenstein 2004).

Population aging in the US will be accompanied by important social changes as well. For example, divorced persons constitute a small proportion of older populations currently, reflecting cohort differences in the likelihood of divorcing. This will soon change in many countries as younger populations with higher rates of divorce and separation enter later life. In the United States, for example, 9% of the 65-and-over population is divorced or separated compared to 17% of people age 55 to 64 and 18 percent of people age 45 to 54 (Manton and Gu 2001). This trend has gender-specific implications: Nonmarried women are less likely than nonmarried men to have accumulated assets and pension wealth for use in later life, and older men are less likely to form and maintain supportive social networks.

To buffer the effects of population aging, one avenue that nations of South and North America are exploring is to shore up public pensions. In developing countries, privately managed savings accounts have been strongly advocated (Estes 2001). Two decades ago, nearly every South American nation had pay-as-you-go systems similar to the Social Security system in the US. Some countries granted civil servants retiring in their age groups of 50+ full salaries for life. Widening budget deficits changed that. In 1981, Chile replaced its public system with retirement accounts funded by worker contributions and managed by private firms. The World Bank encouraged 11 other Latin nations to introduce similar features. For example, in Chile the government addressed its fiscal budget deficit by mobilizing a $49 billion of pension-fund assets that make it easier for companies and corporations to fund investments in the local currency with bond offerings, and most workers have some retirement benefits from this (OECD 2007). At the same time, the downside has been those people who cannot afford a private pension have been left to a low state pension which has intensified poverty (Estes 2001).

For the future, there is no safety guarantee that private pension schemes are protected and pay out for people who invest their savings in such provision. In a de-regulated US pension system, the issue of corporate crime has highlighted the continuing problem of private pension provision. In one example, this was seen clearly with the energy corporation of Enron's embezzlement of billions of dollars of employees private pension schemes (Powell, 2005). This debate amounts to a significant global discourse about pension provision and retirement ages, but one which has largely excluded perspectives which might suggest an enlarged role for the state, and those which might question the stability and cost effectiveness of private schemes.

The International Labour Organisation (ILO) concluded that investing in financial markets is an uncertain and volatile business: that under present pension plans people may save up to 30 percent more than they need, which would reduce their spending during their working life; or they may save 30 percent too little - which would severely cut their spending in retirement (Phillipson, 1998; Estes, Biggs and Phillipson, 2003).

Holtzman (1997), in a paper outlining a World Bank perspective on pension reform, has argued for reducing state pay-as-you-go (PAYG) schemes to a minimal role of basic pension provision. This position has influenced both national governments and transnational bodies, such as the International Labour Organisation (ILO), with the latter now conceding to the World Bank's position with their advocacy of a mean-tested first pension, the promotion of an extended role for individualized and capitalized private pensions, and the call for Organisation for Economic Co- operation and Development (OECD) member countries to raise the age of retirement.

There is also the impact of (Intergovernmental Organizations) IGOs on the pensions debate in Latin America. The IGO is, by definition, an organization with international membership, scope, or presence to provide pension alternatives to that provided by the individual member states in Latin America. The IGOs have sovereign states as their members. Their scope and aims are most usually in the public interest but may also have been created with a specific purpose. The function of such arguments is to create a sense of inevitability and scientific certainty that public pension provision will fail. In so far as this strategy succeeds it creates a self-fulfilling prophecy. If people believe the 'experts' who say publicly sponsored PAYG systems cannot be sustained, they are more likely to act in ways that mean they are unsustainable in practice. Certainly, in Europe and elsewhere, the state pension is an extremely popular institution. To have it removed or curtailed creates massive opposition. Only by controlling the population with the belief that it is demographically unsustainable has room for the private financiers been created and a mass pensions market formed. By 2050, the developing regions of Latin America will find that their populations age 65 and above, as a percentage of the working age population (ages 15-64), will be roughly equivalent to what is found in developed countries today – this is another reason why pensions are becoming a major structural issue for Latin America.

Increasingly, the social infrastructure of welfare states is being targeted as a major area of opportunity for global investors. The World Bank has expressed the belief that the public sector is less efficient in managing new infrastructure activities and that the time has come for private actors to provide what were once assumed to be public services. This view has been strongly endorsed by a variety of multinational companies, especially in their work with the World Trade Organisation (WTO). The WTO enforces more than twenty separate international agreements, using international trade tribunals that adjudicate disputes. Such agreements include the General Agreement on Trade in Services (GATS), the first multilateral legally enforceable agreement covering banking, insurance, financial services and related areas (Estes, Biggs and Phillipson, 2003).

EUROPE

The population structure of western European countries has changed since the turn of the 20th century. Whereas in 1901, just over 6% of the population were at or over age 65, this figure rose steadily reaching 18% in 2001 (Powell, 2005). At the same time, the population of younger people under age 16 fell from 35% to 20%. As European countries reach a relatively high level of population aging, the proportion of workers also tends to decline. European countries, including France, Germany, Greece, Italy, Russia, and the Ukraine, already have seen an absolute decline in the size of their workforce. In countries where tax increases are needed to pay for transfers to growing older populations, the tax burden may discourage future workforce participation. The impact on a Nation's gross domestic product will depend on increases in labor productivity and that State's ability to substitute capital for labor. Less developed countries can shift their economies from labor-intensive to capital-intensive sectors as population aging advances. Options for most European nation states may be more limited. The 'rolling back' of pensions forced through by neo-liberal governments such as Thatcher's administration (1979-91) in the UK was just one symptom of a shift in European history: the 'graying of the baby-boom generation' (Phillipson 1998). The percentage of 60-year-olds and older are growing 1.9% a year in Europe. This is 60% faster than the overall global population. In 1950 there were 12 people aged 15 to 64 to support each one of retirement age. Currently, the global average is nine. It will be only four-to-one by 2050 in Europe (Powell, 2005). By then numbers of older people will outnumber children for the first time. Some economists fear this will lead to bankrupt pensions and lower living standards. It is interesting that in Germany this fear is becoming a battleground for political electioneering. For example, Germany has the largest total population in Europe and the third oldest population in the world, which presents both critical questions on public finances to provide pensions and healthcare and an opportunity for innovations in the marketplace. Currently, aging has started to figure prominently in political discussions prior to 2009 elections, as political parties vie for the elderly vote. The current Merkel administration (2007-) has been criticized for increasing pensions while opponents talk about a "war of generations" requiring young people to pay for taxation for elder care.

Population aging has drawn the further attention across Europe, where the working-age population will decline by 0.6% this in 2010. By 2025 the number of people aged 15 to 64 is projected to dwindle by 10.4% in Spain, 10.7% in Germany and 14.8% in Italy. But aging is just as dramatic in such emerging markets as China - which is expected to have 265 million 65-year-olds by 2020 - and Russia and Ukraine (Cook and Powell, 2007).

Using evidence from the UK, the percentage of people of working age, that is 16-64, is projected to drop from 64% in 1994 to 58% in 2031 (Powell, 2005). As the number of workers per pensioner decreases there will be pressure on pension provision. This is evident now, in such areas of pensions and long term care, the retreat of the state made evident in the erosion of State Earnings Related Pay are forcing people to devise their own strategies for economic survival in old age (Phillipson 1998). In the British context that also impinges on global societies in general, private pensions are slowly being introduced in order to prevent the 'burden' of an aging population. These are ways in which the State continues to rely on apocalyptic projections such as 'demographic time bomb' about aging populations in order to justify cuts in public expenditure (Powell 2005). Hence, the population of Great Britain, like that of other European countries, is aging rapidly. There are only enough young people to fill one in three of the new and replacement jobs that will need to be taken up over the next decade (Powell 2005). Older people take much of the responsibility for our social and civic life and for the care of children, the sick and the very old in the community. Yet the gap between wealth and poverty, choice and the absence of choice for older people is stark and growing wider (Phillipson 1998).

AFRICA

Economic security, health and disability, and living conditions in later life are policy concerns throughout the world, but the nature of the problem differs considerably from continent to continent and between and within countries – especially within Africa.

In Africa older people make up a relatively small fraction of the total population, and traditionally their main source of support has been the household and family, supplemented in many cases by other informal mechanisms, such as kinship networks and mutual aid societies. In 2005, Nigeria ranked among the top 30 countries in the world on the basis of the size of its population age 60 and over. Nigeria had the largest older population in sub-Saharan Africa, with over 6 million people age 60 and over; South Africa had just over 3.4 million. Congo and South Africa are projected to have nearly 5 million older people in 2030. Burkina Faso, Cameroon, Cote d'Ivoire, Madagascar, Mozambique, Niger, Senegal, and Uganda are all projected to have their older populations grow to over one million people by 2030 (Building Blocks 2004). There is very little careful empirical research has been undertaken on long-term trends in the welfare of older people, there are a number of reasons to believe that traditional caring and social support mechanisms in Africa are under increasing strain (OECD 2007).

African economies, among the poorest in the world, are still heavily dependent on subsistence agriculture, and average income per capita is now lower than it was at the end of the 1960s. Consequently, the region contains a growing share of the world's poor. In addition, reductions in fertility and child mortality have meant that, despite the huge impact of the HIV/AIDS epidemic across much of the region, both the absolute size and the proportion of the population age 60 and over have grown and will continue to grow over the next 30 years (Estes, Biggs and Phillipson 2003).

In Africa, older people have traditionally been viewed in a positive light, as repositories of information and wisdom. And while African families are generally still intact, social and economic changes taking place can weaken traditional social values and networks that provide care and support in later life. Africa has long carried a high burden of disease, including from malaria and tuberculosis; today it is home to more than 60% of all people living with HIV—some 25.8 million in 2005. The vast majority of those affected are still in their prime wage-earning years, at an age when, normally, they would be expected to be the main wage earners and principal sources of financial and material support for older people and children in their families. Many older people have had to deal with the loss of their own support while absorbing the additional responsibilities of caring for their orphaned grandchildren. Increasingly, then, it appears that African societies are being asked to cope with population aging with neither a comprehensive formal social security system nor a well-functioning traditional care system in place (Building Blocks 2004).

The big issue is that a majority of the world's population of older people (61 per cent, or 355 million) live in poorer African countries. This proportion will increase to nearly 70 percent by 2025. For many countries, however, population aging has been accompanied by reductions in per capita income and declining living standards. Epstein (2001) notes that between 1950 and the late 1970s, life expectancy increased by least 10 percent in every developing country in the world, or on average by about 15 years. However, at the beginning of the twenty-first century, life expectancy remains below fifty in more than ten developing countries, and since 1970 has actually fallen, or has barely risen in a number of African countries (Phillipson 1998).

The AIDS epidemic is certainly a major factor here, but development loans requiring the privatization of health care have also had an impact. Epstein (2001) reports, for example, that by the mid- 1990s the African continent was transferring four times more in debt repayment than it spent on health or education. More generally, Help Age International (2000: 8) argue that:

> 'Older people's poverty is still not a core concern in the social, economic and ethical debates of our time. Their right to development is routinely denied, with aging seen as a minority interest or case for special pleading. Poverty and social exclusion remain the main stumbling blocks to the realisation of the human rights of older people worldwide.'

Africa, Europe and the Americas have revealed some of the consequences of populational aging. Before we explore China, there are some major shifts taken place in other countries in Asia. Kim and Lee (2007) claim the growing older adult population is beginning to exert pressure on the East Asian countries economies. Three decades ago, major industrialized countries had begun to grapple with the similar problem. With increasing reductions in fertility rates, more East Asian economies such as Japan, Hong Kong, South Korea, Singapore and Taiwan are expected to turn into "super-aging societies" by 2025 (Kim and Lee 2007). However, the magnitude of the future impact depends on the (in)ability of individual economies to resolve the demographic burden through changes such as increased pension reform, immigration policy and extension of retirement age. Like western countries, Asia will ultimately have to tackle issues related to pension reform and the provision of long term health care services (Cook and Powell, 2007).

Japan faces an enormous challenge due to population aging trends. Already, 17 of every 100 of its people are over 65, and this ratio will near 30 in 15 years. From 2005 to 2012, Japan's workforce is projected to shrink by around 1% each year - a pace that will accelerate after that. Economists fear that, besides straining Japan's underfunded pension system (Cook and Powell, 2007), the decline of workers and young families will make it harder for Japan to generate new wealth.

The future challenge of providing for the older adults population is especially urgent in the world's two biggest nations - India and China (Kim and Lee 2007). Only 11% of Indians have pensions, and they tend to be civil servants and the affluent. With a young population and relatively big families, many of the older adult population still count on their children for support. Relying on family support will be even more difficult in China as the population continues to age. By 2030 in China, there will be only two working-age people to support every retiree. Yet only 20% of workers have government- or company-funded pensions or medical coverage (Cook and Powell, 2007). This has huge implications for China and the life course.

Chapter 3

AGE, PROFESSIONAL POWER AND SOCIAL POLICY IN THE UNITED KINGDOM

This chapter examines the interrelationship between old age, professional power, and social policy. In particular, dominant theoretical models in social gerontology are reviewed and an alternative framework for understanding social gerontological issues—Foucauldian gerontology-- is advanced. Foucauldian narratives are employed to delineate the historical relationship between professional social work and recent social policy for older people in the United Kingdom. In addition, by employing a Foucauldian framework to interrogate identity formation, professional practices, and policy narratives, enriches and widens the disciplinary subject matter of theorizing aging studies. The structure of this article is in three parts: The review of old-age theories with an introduction of Foucault's potential contribution to gerontological analysis, the historical overview of the instigation of professional intervention in modernity and the changing roles and responsibilities in relation to older people utilizing Foucault's (1977) genealogical method, and the exploration and application of Foucault's key notion of governmentality (1977; Rose & Miller, 1992) in the analysis of social policy for older people. As we go beyond the fin-de-siècle, ageism, reinforces the predominantly perverse yet embedded and calculated perceptions of old age present in western society. Old age throughout last century was seen as a social problem (Stott, 1981; Townsend, 1981; Walker, 1981) and this predominant perspective is still reiterated through the narratives used by policy makers, mass media, and social gerontologists on all sides of the Atlantic.

Hence, the narrative of aging into old age still begins and ends with the problematization of economic, social, and physical decline. In Western culture in particular the aging body is the bottom line, subject to relentless decay (Stott, 1981; Powell, 2000). Insofar as there is a history of aging, there is also a history of efforts to control, supervise, and regulate older people (Powell & Biggs, 2000). The master narrative of natural decline of aging bodies hides the location of complex intersections of negative ideas which comprise an aging culture (Biggs & Powell, 1999; Longino & Powell, forthcoming). In terms of physical and social and economic power, old age is seen as a write-off. The adverse quality of life experienced by many older people caused by capitalism is well documented (Phillipson, 1982; Townsend, 1981) as are the positive images of old age (Blaikie, 1999; Gilleard & Higgs, 2001).

Yet, in the 1980s in particular, we have seen a steady growth of popularized discourses, characteristic of publications of Anglo-American research studies, which have attempted to describe the social condition of older people as a 'burden' and a 'demographic time bomb' while touching upon social gerontology (Phillipson & Walker, 1986; Townsend, 1981; Walker, 1981). Such critical research in social gerontology, while important, tends to over emphasize either the social problems of older people or more negatively, older people as a social problem.

Coupled with this critical research, there has also been a huge rise in interest and debate about aging in relation to social policy in the United Kingdom, despite the charge that the subject of aging has been neglected in policy discourse (Bury, 1995; Biggs & Powell, 2001). Phillipson and Walker (1986) did note a close connection of old age with social policy and despite this, much of the work in the aging field has been therefore policy oriented, and indeed policy driven (Gilleard & Higgs, 2001), as successive Conservative and New Labour governments have attempted to address the never-ending crises and problems that an aging population appears to create in the United Kingdom.

As a consequence, developing and analyzing the triangularized relationship of aging, professional social work practice, and social policy has remained *theoretically* underdeveloped, as an apparently applied field of study has remained silent. Yet, "all three have contributed to the transformation of aging from a natural process into a social problem" (Butler, 1975, p. 146). Fennell et al. (1988) comment, for example, that theoretical developments in social facets of aging have at best had a "chequered history" (p. 41). The contribution of wide social theory to a specific understanding of old age, professional social work, and social policy has been quite limited despite notable exceptions (Phillipson, 1998; Biggs, 1999; Biggs & Powell, 2001; Powell & Biggs, 2000). Among writers in mainstream British sociology the major works of sociological texts have ignored the topic of old age altogether (see Giddens, 1987, 1990) and this has even been replicated in the discipline of mainstream British social policy (see Williams, 1994; Alcock, 1996) which has focused exclusive analysis upon race, class, and gender to the exclusion of age as an identity variable. Perhaps, the major sociological issue and lesson to be learnt is how to overcome the triumvirate of class, race, and gender without merely adding an increasing list of identity formations such as sexuality, disability, and age.

We need to question how old age has been theorized. Different sociological theories of old age are concerned with the social significance of age. Some are concerned with the individual's adjustment to growing older and others are concerned with the relative distribution of material disadvantage of older people. There is a somewhat heterogeneous bundle of theoretical disciplines, each with different concerns, strengths, and weaknesses.

THE DISCIPLINARY FOCUS OF OLD AGE

The rise and consolidation of social theories and philosophies of old age can be traced to the concern about the consequences of demographic change and the potential shortage of younger workers in the early post-war years in the United Kingdom and United States. Social gerontology emerged as a disciplinary study, which attempted to respond to the social policy ramifications of demographic change (Vincent, 1996). The subject matter of social gerontology was shaped by significant external forces: first, by government intervention to achieve specific outcomes in social and health policy and second, by a political and economic environment which viewed an aging population as creating a social problem for society. This has generated the attention of modernist orthodoxies in recent years spanning functionalist, Marxist, and feminist ideas. However, in the 1950s and 1960s, it was the functionalist philosophy which dominated the gerontological landscape in the United States. Indeed, functionalist philosophies of aging often mirror the norms and values of their creators and their social times, reflecting culturally dominant views of what should be the appropriate way to analyze social phenomena (Longino & Powell, forthcoming). The two theories contrasted here follow this normative pattern. Both functionalist schools of disengagement and activity theories postulate not only how individual behavior changes with aging but also imply how it should change.

FUNCTIONALIST ANALYSIS OF OLD AGE

There are two broad schools of thought within the functionalist umbrella theory: Disengagement theory and Activity theory. Disengagement theory is associated with Cumming and Henry (1961) and proposes that gradual withdrawal of older people from work roles and social relationships is both an inevitable and natural process. "Withdrawal may be accompanied from the outset by an increased preoccupation with himself: certain institutions may make it easy for him" (p. 14).

Such withdrawal prepares society, the individual older person, and those with whom s/he had personal relationships for death—the ultimate disengagement (Cumming & Henry, 1961). The process of this variant of functionalism benefits society because the death of individual society members does not prevent the ongoing functioning of the social system (Powell, 2000).

Activity theory emphasizes age roles and a concern for the adaptation of people to old age (Neugarten, 1996). Activity theory is a counterpoint to Disengagement theory with its claim that a successful old age can be achieved by maintaining roles and relationships. The Activity theory maintains that any loss of roles, activities, or relationships within old age should be replaced by new roles or activities to ensure happiness, value consensus, and well-being.

A number of critiques exist: First, Activity theory condones indifference towards old age and social problems (Bond & Coleman, 1990). Second, Disengagement theory underplays the role cultural and economic structures have in creating the intentional consequence of withdrawal. This theory engages in sociological reductionism in presupposing that old age is defined entirely by the explanation of disengagement and engages in functional teleology in attempting to explain old age in terms of its effects or death (Powell, 2000). Such approaches underemphasize the active subjectivity of individuals and the meanings and interpretations placed by them upon age relations. Activity theory neglects issues of power, inequality, and conflict between age groups. An apparent value consensus may reflect the interests of dominant groups within society who find it advantageous to have age power relations organized in such a way (Longino & Powell, forthcoming; Powell, 2001). It is the very notion of power and the unequal distribution of resources which prompted the emergence of a critical gerontology research in the United States and United Kingdom.

POLITICAL ECONOMY OF OLD AGE

For Estes, Swan, and Gerard (1982), social class in the United States is perceived as the master narrative and determinant of the position of older people in capitalist society. This grand theory, drawn from Marxian historiography, locates the determining explanatory factors in the structure of society and focuses upon welfare and its contribution to the institutional de-commodification of retired older people. Negative attitudes towards older people and social position are best explained by the loss of social worth brought about by their loss of productive roles in a society that puts premium and policy emphasis on economic production (Estes et al., 1982).

This is an argument reiterated by critical gerontological writers in the United Kingdom on the social position of older people. Townsend (1981) observes that society creates the social problems of old age through structured dependency such as, social practices embedded in institutional agism, lack of material resources via poverty, retirement policies, negative consequences of residential care, and passive forms of community care services. Compounding this, Walker (1981) argued for a political economy of old age in order to understand the position of older people. In particular, Walker (1981) paid attention to the social creation of dependency and how social structure and relations espoused by the mode of production help intensify structural class marginalization. In a similar vein, Phillipson (1982, 1986) also considers how capitalism helps construct the social marginality of older people in key areas such as welfare delivery. Unlike the functionalist accounts, the important argument to be made is that inequalities in the distribution of resources should be understood in relation to the distribution of power within society rather than in terms of individual variation.

Despite its critical appeal, this theory raises a number of questions. According to Turner (1989) such an approach over concentrates analysis of the treatment of older people in terms of class relations within capitalist societies and neglects differences between capitalist societies in the treatment of older people (Blakemore & Boneham, 1994). More recently, attention has been paid to ways in which capitalist societies structure age relations in terms of gender (Arber & Ginn, 1991, 1995) and to race and ethnicity (Blakemore & Boneham, 1994). Indeed, this theoretical approach homogenizes and reifies older age by discounting potential for improvements in the social situation of older people (Featherstone & Hepworth, 1993; Gilleard & Higgs, 2001). Hence, for some researchers the complexity of social life is more of a continuous, never-ending project with variable outcomes than the Political Economy theory gives credence (Giddens, 1991).

FEMINIZATION OF OLD AGE

Although in recent years there has been a small but growing body of evidence in mainstream sociological theory, the interconnection of age and gender has been under-theorized and overlooked (Arber & Ginn, 1995). Mainstream refers to dominant theories in the sociological field such as functionalist and Marxist theory that could be accused of being gender blind. As Arber and Ginn (1995) point out – there exists a tiny handful of feminist writers who take the topic of age seriously in understanding gender. Arber and Ginn (1991) claim patriarchal society exercises power through the chronologies of employment and reproduction, and through the sexualized promotion of a youthful appearance in women. As a result, many older women suffer from double jeopardy through age and sexual discrimination. In terms of United Kingdom demographic profiles there are predominantly many more older women than older men (Arber & Ginn, 1991) which is substantiated by official statistics: "In 1995 there were 3.0 million men and 3.8 million women aged 65-79 and 0.7 million men and 1.6 million women aged over 80" (Age Concern England, 1997, p. 16).

Women have unequal access to community care services (Hughes, 1995) which is differentiated by issues of race (Dominelli, 1997) and disability. Older women's high visibility as service users of community care services has been highlighted by much research in feminist gerontology (Arber & Ginn, 1995; Dalley, 1988). The work of Finch (1989) has problematized the construction of services for older people by describing how services contribute to dominant constructions of older people, the majority of whom are women, as helpless, incapable, and dependent. Discourses of power not only define old age but also act as a powerful instrument for dividing aging experiences for both women and men.

Taken together, these different theories have helped shape debate about the extent and nature of an aging society. However, the concerns of these theoretical resources have been primarily macro-oriented; for example, according to Gilleard and Higgs (2001) the Political Economy approach overemphasizes structural disadvantage or structured dependency at the expense of attention to older people's agency in resisting poverty and low status through social organization; macro-level analysis neglects cultural change as well as the diversity of cultural meanings among older people and renders the voice of older people inaudible (Blaikie, 1999; Gilleard & Higgs, 2001). Indeed, over twenty years ago though still relevant to the advancing theoretical advancements today, Kalish (1979) offers a devastating critique of the expert models of aging:

> "We" understand how badly you are being treated, that "we" have the tools to improve your treatment…You are poor, lonely, weak, incompetent and ineffectual. You are sick, in need of better housing and transportation and "we"…are finally going to turn our attention to you, the deserving elderly. (p. 398)

Unfortunately, such sociological theories that focus upon the social problems of older people may have promoted the agism of which many are arguing against. Contradicting Hockey and James's (1993) conceptualization of old age, old age as a term can no longer be used to describe and homogenise the experiences of people spanning an age range of 30 to 40 years. "The pace of cohort differentiation has speeded up, with different age groups reflecting cohort differences in life chances that are created by period specific conditions, policies and economic transformations" (Conrad, 1992, p. 72). Hence, there is differentiation of subjective experiences of aging in the lifestyles of older people (Gilleard & Higgs, 2001). In recent years, the importance of subjectivity in gerontology has taken a new and important direction with the development of postmodern theories of aging identity (Featherstone & Hepworth, 1993; Blaikie, 1999). This, according to Katz (1996) has led to a significant skewing of gerontological theorizing and the relative failure of more broadly based social and life course approaches such as functionalist narratives to impinge upon modernist thinking about old age. However, there have been some important exceptions to this trend, most notably in attempts to develop a humanistic gerontology (Cole et al., 1992) and analysis focusing around postmodernity on aging identity (Featherstone & Wernick, 1995) based primarily in the United States and United Kingdom academies. The next section introduces the work of Foucault and seeks to add a new theoretical dimension for understanding social gerontology.

FOUCAULT AND OLD AGE:
A NEW DOMAIN OF THEORIZING AGING

> The theories Foucault devised are not intended as permanent structures, enduring in virtue of their universal truth. They are temporary scaffoldings, erected for a specific purpose, which Foucault is happy to abandon to whomever might find them useful. (Gutting, 1994, p. 16)

The work of Michel Foucault has significance to the processes of old age in two respects. First, his analyses of power have relevance older people's experiences. Foucault describes how the patient, the madman, and the criminal are constructed through disciplinary techniques, for example, the "medical gaze" (1973, p. 29). Older people's relationships with professional social workers could be constructed in similar ways (Powell & Biggs, 2000).

Second, Foucault (1977) offers a methodology that examines both the official discourses on social policy and the social workers and older people operating within these discourses. It is necessary to become conscious of the institutionalized practices in terms of which old age is constituted in order to broaden the scope for political action.

Introducing Foucauldian Gerontology

Until recently, there has been little serious Foucauldian study of aging and critical theorists relied on a limited number of sources in the work of American and Canadian writers such as Katz (1996) and more recently, from writers in the United Kingdom (Biggs & Powell, 1999 and 2001; Powell &

Biggs, 2000; Powell & Cook, 2000 and 2001; Wahidin & Powell, 2001). These writers have been influenced by Foucault's interest in the way in which individuals are constructed as social subjects, knowable through disciplines and discourses. The key aim of Foucault's work has been "to create a history of the different modes by which, in our culture human beings are made subjects" (1982, p. 208). In The *Birth of the Clinic* (1973) and *Madness and Civilization* (1967), Foucault traces changes in the ways in which physical deterioration was discussed which has obvious implications for gerontology. Foucault utilizes the distinctive methodology of archaeology for these studies that aims to provide a "history of statements that claim the status of truth" (Davidson, 1986, p. 221). Foucault's later work, *Discipline and Punish* (1977) focuses on the techniques of power that operate within an institution and simultaneously create "a whole domain of knowledge and a whole type of power" (p. 185). This work is characterized as genealogy and examines the "political regime of the production of truth" (Davidson, 1986, p. 224). Both archaeology and genealogy are concerned with the limits and conditions of discourses but the latter takes into account political and economic concerns (Shumway, 1989). Drawing from the work of Foucault, Powell and Biggs (2000) highlighted how medical narratives of decline and deterioration are discourses that have attempted to colonize definitions afforded to aging experiences. Coupled with this, Powell and Biggs (2000) have illustrated how professional power has dominated social relationships with older people. Professionals such as gerontologists and geriatricians are pivotal interventionists in social relations and in the coordination of social arrangements, pursue a power to classify and pathologize with consequences for the reproduction of knowledge about aging and simultaneous maintenance of power relations (Powell & Biggs, 2000).

When applied to the experience of becoming old, a Foucauldian theory of gerontology can be constitutive of old age because individuals are both the objects and subjects of professional power/knowledge (Smart, 1985) and because it also provides a space for the dissemination of particular techniques of surveillance such as social work.

A History of the Present: The Rise of Social Work with Older People

Foucault (1977) was principally interested in how particular forms of knowledge came into existence and the social conditions that made this possible. This section draws from this genealogical argument and sketches the main developments of social work by "digging" into the past in order to explain present social practices.

The emergence and consolidation of professional social work in modernity is associated with the transformations that took place in the nineteenth century around a series of anxieties about the family (Jones, 1983). Coupled with this, social work between the public and private spheres was produced by new relations between the politico-legal institutions of law, administration, medicine, and school. Thus, social work developed as a halfway point between the individual identity and the branches of government, which would be in danger of taking responsibility for everybody's needs and hence would undermine the liberal hegemonic discourse of responsibility of the family (Biggs & Powell, 2001).

Over the past fifty years in particular, social workers have turned to the human and social sciences that have been dominant via professional practice and applied their insights and explanations to social problems and problem people. Social work, therefore, was formed in the project of modernity based on Enlightenment notions of progress and bringing social order to family lives.

In modernity, social work as a form of social control was characterized the processes of normalization, discipline, and surveillance (Foucault 1977; Powell & Biggs, 2000) originally linked with the development of the modern prison but increasingly reflected in diffuse use of surveillance via the school, the hospital, the family, and the community (Foucault, 1977). Hence, institutions of surveillance have become increasingly blurred. The central focus of modern social systems of surveillance was the governmental classification of the elderly population based on the scientific claims of different experts in science and medicine (Powell & Biggs, 2000).

For Foucault (1973, p. 105) the expert "gaze" constructs individuals as both subjects and objects of knowledge and power. As Powell and Biggs (2000) point out: 'The identities of elderly people and old age have been constructed through expert discourses of 'decay' and 'deterioration' and the 'gaze' helps to intensify regulation over older people in order to normalize and provide treatment for such notions" (p. 7).

Techniques of surveillance are so sophisticated, argues Foucault that "inspection functions ceaselessly. The gaze is everywhere" (1977, p. 195). Foucault points here to the means through which power is exercised. He places the processes of discipline, surveillance, individualization, and normalization at the center of his analysis. These processes were key elements in the genesis of public welfare agencies from the instigation of the welfare state in 1945. For example, social work with older people was part of a strategy that extended "control over minutiae of the conditions of life and conduct" (Cousins & Hussain, 1984, p. 146). Within this discourse the professional social worker became "the great advisor and expert" (Rabinow, 1984, pp. 283-4) in the utilization of scientific-medico insights in constructing services for older people.

The notion of risk is fundamental to the way experts experience and organize the social world. Risk assessment is crucial to the understanding and control of the future (Beck, 1992). The central yet uncertain nature of risk and risk assessment is pivotal to understanding the changing nature and role of power/knowledge and experts in contemporary society (Beck, 1992). Risks come into being where traditions and assumed values such as psychoanalysis have deteriorated. As Beck (1992) states: "The concept of risk is like a probe which permits us over and over again to investigate the entire construction plan, as well as every individual speck of cement in the structure of civilization" (p. 176).

The emergence of a risk society arises because of the undermining and loss of faith concerning power/knowledge and hierarchies of truth and expert systems. It is not by chance, then, that the increased focus on risk in social work coincided with the decline in trust in social workers' expertise, decision-making, and scientific-medico insights and the growing reliance on increasingly complex systems of care managerialism.

FROM SOCIAL WORK TO CARE MANAGEMENT

It is evident that the role of social work has changed from a service-orientated approach to one of assessment of individual need and care management embodying principles of empowerment and choice (Dept. of Health, 1989; Levick, 1992). However, the interpersonal elements of professional power including the social relationships have been reduced with, instead, a greater emphasis on the management of older clients (Walker, 1993; Biggs & Powell, 2001). Gabe (1991) argues that the Griffiths Report (1988) in the United Kingdom made no reference to social workers at all and already the concept role of care manager is of common use in policy discourse. Care managers are simultaneously entrepreneurial and creative in the way they plan and meet objectives (Clarke, 1994). Care managers therefore have to meet need and ration resources at the same time which raises the question: Is there a large gap between needs and resources.

The rise and of the care manager has marked a fundamental shift from the social work practitioner to a consolidated, managerial role and occupational identity. In managerial positions, judgment is increasingly bound up with managerial imperatives concerning corporate objectives and resource control (Flynn, 1992). The devolution of managerial responsibilities is intended to empower individuals and to constrain professional autonomy by having such care managers internalize budgetary disciplines and translate social policy imperatives. These imperatives have had a huge impact upon old age and professional power.

SOCIAL POLICY FOR OLDER PEOPLE IN THE UNITED KINGDOM

Since the 1960s there have been increasing calls for more community care in the United Kingdom. The ambiguity of this notion meant that it was an important objective of both conservative and liberal political parties. In the 1970s, both conservative and labor governments promoted deinstitutionalization of care and argued that community care was a way of supporting those individuals who found it difficult to be self-sufficient and lead independent lives (Moroney, 1976).

By the 1980s community care became a popular slogan by the government to promote its reform of welfare provision. The conservative government in 1981 made their intention clear with the White Paper Care in the Community (DHSS, 1981). One of its central recommendations was to become practice via the policy "care in the community must increasingly mean care by the community" (DHSS, 1981, p. 3). This articulated a change in the role of public sector. In 1984 Norman Fowler claimed the principal role of the state was to "back up and develop the assistance which is given by private and voluntary support" (1984, p. 3). Coupled with Fowler's comments the *Audit Commission* (1986) report *Making a Reality of Community Care* argued too many people were being cared for in institutions. Community care in this report was interpreted as a means by which public provision of services would become less important. The notion of wider choice held by the *Griffiths Report* (1988) for older people to exercise some influence over care packages was reiterated by the White Paper (1989) *Caring for People. Choice* is defined as "giving people a greater individual say in how they live their lives and the services they need to help them" (Dept. of Health, 1989, p. 4). This was to be met via care managerialism and greater welfare pluralism of formal, informal, voluntary, and private modes for older people. The community care reforms were not simply about restructuring organizations but also about changing cultures-- replacing the public service ethic with a mixed economy of welfare (Clarke, 1994).

In 1990 with the introduction of the NHS and Community Care Act, there has been a reassessment of the role afforded to individual choice in the delivery of social welfare in the United Kingdom (Dept. of Health, 1991). It is further supposed that if individuals are given effective choices they will prompt providers of services into the operative incorporation of the three *e's* of efficient, effective, and economical responses while guaranteeing consumer sovereignty (Clarke, 1994). The intellectualism for this ideology comes from neoliberalism (Rose & Miller, 1992). From the 1980s a state emerged based upon minimal intervention and regulation via a rolling program of privatization, deregulation, and contraction of services. Within the mixed economy of welfare, there has been the social construction of a market- orientated, consumer-based approach to the delivery of care and the role of older people as consumers. As Sim (1987) et al. claim the state is being reorganized to include a retention of a strong center to formulate policy but the dissemination of responsibility for policy implementation to a wide range of private, public, and informal modes.

A Foucauldian Analysis of Social Policy for Older People: The Case of the NHS and Community Care Act

In endeavouring to understand recent changes in the form and impact of examples of the NHS and Community Care Act (1990) for older people in the United Kingdom, Foucault's (1978) concept of governmentality provides a useful analytical framework. This concept makes fundamental connections between structural processes and agency and has been used to characterise features of contemporary, neoliberal government (Rose & Miller 1992) in the United Kingdom. A core element of neoliberal governance is an emphasis on enterprise as an individual and corporate strategy and on its concomitant discourse of marketization much exemplified by the genesis of the NHS and Community Care Act (1990) which embodies value for money and transference of public expenditure to new areas of private welfare pluralism for older people (Dept. of Health, 1989).

The Foucauldian Notion of Governmentality

According to Foucault (qtd. in Burchell et al., 1991) governmentality comprises three tiers: it is the result of transformations within the modern state; it is a tendency to institutionalize a particular form of power, and it is the "ensemble formed by institutions, procedures, analyses and reflections . . . calculations and tactics" (pp. 102-3) that enable the exercise of power directed towards the regulation of a population (older people) using various (care management) apparatuses of security.

For Foucault (1978) government is concerned with the 'conduct of conduct', and neo-liberal government is especially concerned with inculcating a new set of values and objectives orientated towards incorporating individual older people as both players and partners in a marketized system. In such a regime older people are exhorted, indeed expected, to become entrepreneurs in all spheres and to accept responsibility for the management of risk (Beck, 1992); older people then govern themselves. For neotheory and community care act as an extension of such philosophy in practice, older people are very much cast as social actors in the market place, mobilizing selectivity of services in the light of care managerial assessment of services.

Coupled with this, Rose and Miller argue, we must investigate political rationalities and technologies of government, "the complex of mundane programmes, calculations, techniques, apparatuses, documents and procedures through which authorities seek to embody and give effect to governmental ambitions" (1992, p. 175). Technologies of government consist of complex devices and practices through which social groups such as care managers attempt to operationalize, following Rose and Miller, their program of tailoring "packages of care" for older people (Dept. of Health, 1994, p. 11). This could include community care assessment and professionalization (care management) and by implication, the elaborate paraphernalia of contract services. Such technologies, Rose and Miller (1992) suggest, articulate and deploy political rationalities, and thereby enable action-at-a-distance.

There are a number of distinguishing but paradoxical aspects of neoliberal government. First, while there is increasing dependence on professional expertise, there is also a drive to make, for example, older people active participants in their own rule via empowerment (Dept. of Health, 1989). One of the ways of facilitating both is the representation of issues as nonpolitical so that expert knowledge becomes dominant in "rendering the complexities of modern social and economic life knowable, practicable and amenable to governing" (Johnson, 1995, p. 23). Again this was crystallized in the White Paper (1989) Caring for People which promoted social service departments as "enabling authorities" both facilitating care management in constructing "packages of care" and "empowering" older people with "choice" of services via the process of "assessment" (Dept. of Health, 1989, pp. 4-14).

Furthermore, there is a multiplication of sources and types of authority and a proliferation of agencies in social care, so that "so many of those who are subjects of authority in one field play a part in its exercise in others" (Rose, 1993, p. 287). In neoliberal regimes there is also an apparent dispersal of power (Cousins & Hussain, 1984) achieved through establishing structures in which care managers and older people as consumers are coopted into or coproduce governance through their own accountable and regulated choices. As Burchell (1993) observes this is directly connected with the political rationality which assigns primacy to marketization and the autonomization of society in which the paradigm of economic action and enterprise culture comes to dominate *all* forms of conduct including those areas formerly regarded as noncommercial such as community care services.

It is the non-commercial area that needs more detailed exploration and empirical focus, especially within the social service departmental institutions of the British welfare state. The very significance of auto-nomization is that the state appears to relinquish direct control over the actions of public agencies and social policy through a strategy of privatization and insertion of exchange relationships that commodify and monetarize nonmarket welfare goods and services (Burchell, 1993). In other words, there is a strategic aim to diffuse the public sector's monolithic power to encourage diversity and fragmentation of provision from public, private, voluntary, and informal modes that is an embodiment of the neoliberalism policy of maximizing choice for individuals. Such a strategy, as Rose and Miller (1992) observe, constitutes a fundamental transformation in the mechanisms for governing social life, as it has resulted not only in a rhetorical but a material outcome in their pervasiveness of market disciplines and their objectives of effectiveness, efficiency and economy. To paraphrase the Griffiths Report (1988): place older people's services under the management of a care manager who purchases services from either private or public agencies.

Marketization thus entails the simultaneous encouragement of consumerism and dependency, the expansion of budgeting and managerial discourse, and structures of accountability in which care management expertise is problematized in new ways. Such technologies of government displace earlier forms with new rationalities of contracts and competition whereby professionals participate in governmentality yet at the same time are themselves subject to intensified forms of regulation and control (Rose, 1993). This leads some care managers to leave their jobs due to extra pressures such as budget devolving and allocation (Hughes, 1995).

As Du Gay (1996) has observed, enterprise is a dominant discourse of government and it has permeated innumerable policies spanning from social welfare to health from the 1980s to the present. Moreover, it has combined two interlinked developments: a stress on the necessity for enterprising subjects or what Burchell terms "responsibilization" (1993, p. 276) and the resolution of central state control with individual and organizational autonomy through service provision, each of which has redefined previous patterns of social relationships within welfare agencies and between those agencies and their older customers/clients. However, while acknowledging the introduction of neoliberal policies to stimulate market modes of action, it is important to recognize, as Burchell (1993) points out, that the implementation of a community care is varied, highly contingent, and uncertain. In addition, "the forms of action constructed for schools, hospitals, general practitioners, housing estates, prisons and other social forms are new, invented, and clearly not a simple extension or reproduction of already existing economic forms of action" (p. 275).

Consequently, there are compelling reasons to examine and recognize varying patterns and contingent outcomes of social policies. In doing this, we may arrive at a less all- encompassing, deterministic, and antireductionist conception of governmentality. While some commentators claim that Foucault rejected monolithic images of the state (Smart, 1985), characterised neoliberal government technologies as pluralizing, and conceptualized discipline and power as forms of domination in which subjects are active, governmentality as an analytical construct remains a highly abstract metaphor for a complex and heterogeneous series of interrelated social practices and institutional structures. Like any theoretical, ideal type it may not necessarily claim empirical validity if it is to be used in explaining the implementation facets of community care policy.

EXAMPLES OF IMPLEMENTING POLICY AND PRACTICE FOR OLDER PEOPLE

Studies of experiences of the implementation of the community care (Hughes, 1995; Henwood, 1995) reforms, namely, the NHS and Community Care Act (1990), indicate that mechanisms of control and regulation are not simply problematic at policy level, but are deeply institutionalized and embedded in the context and quality of service delivery and professional practice. The NHS and Community Care Act (1990) (Dept. of Health, 1991, 1994) has much in common with Lindblom's "incrimentalism"(qtd. in Flynn, 1992, p.) where budgeting of resources for services follows a comprehensive process of analysing policy objectives, prioritizing competing objectives, and evaluating means, a "muddling through" (Lindblom qtd. in Flynn, 1992, pp. 26-29) perspective. Such incrementalism exemplifies much variability in terms of decision-making for older people and family care. Walker (1993), reiterating earlier arguments from Gillian Dalley (1988), claims that there was already evidence to illuminate that the development of services had resulted in greater formalization of informal networks or compulsory altruism (Dalley, 1988) of family care for older people. Although, research has shown that professional confidence in familism is sometimes misplaced, family care can be both the best and the worst form of support (Qureshi & Walker, 1989; Biggs & Powell, 2000).

Further still, while the nexus of services in the welfare state has increased in scale and totality (Johnson, 1995), it becomes apparent that the more complex and indeterminate the service, the more difficult it is to monitor and evaluate the satisfaction felt by those receiving the service (Hughes, 1995) which in itself marginalizes the very *experience* of community care to politically indeterminate and individually safe questions about the level of satisfaction of services from care managers. As Glennerster and Lewis (1996) found in their study of social care, the purchaser/provider split resulted in a period of tension and mutual suspicion, an increase in bureaucratization (which threatened to become an end in itself), adversarial relationships, and increased distance between senior managers and frontline workers. Similarly, Deakin (1996) reports that in the quasimarket for community care, there was little sign of the emergence of long-term stability, partnership, or even trust. Further, Deakin (1996) noted that efforts by purchasers to minimize risk led them to develop *both* loose and tight strategies of market management resulting in contingent, ambiguous, and contradictory patterns. To paraphrase Lindblom (qtd. in Flynn, 1992) these social actors are "still muddling, not yet through."

Even in the United Kingdom private sector there has been a problem of gaining enough older clients for a particular service. A survey of the United Kingdom Home Care Association (HCA), an organization of private domiciliary services, highlighted that 23% of its members had only 20 clients when a minimum of 40 clients were needed (Tinker, 1997) to make the business or aging enterprise (Estes, 1979) viable. By applying the profit motive to care management and welfare pluralism will this mean financial questions take precedence over human regimes with welfare technologies taking precedence over human contact?

Such empirical examples are also potential sources of instability and contingency in the process of governmentality. Governmentality may be a totalizing discourse but in practice it is complex and differentiated, dynamic and fluid. It needs to be thought of as permanently incomplete and dependent on an enormously diffuse system of action which itself is the aggregate or structural effect of innumerable interpersonal and organizational transactions. There seems a strong argument for linking Foucauldian notions of governmentality with, and building on, ideas derived from a Political Economy sociology. Granovetter (1985) criticized both conventional, undersocialized, economistic and oversocialized, sociological accounts of action, and stressed the importance of socially embedded networks as a way of theorizing relations between macrostructures and microlevels of action. Thus:

> Actors do not behave or decide as atoms outside a social context, nor do they adhere slavishly to a script written for them by the intersection of social categories that they happen to occupy. Their attempts at purposive action are instead embedded in concrete, ongoing systems of social relations. (Granovetter, 1985, p. 487)

In Granovetter's sociology, economic institutions or aging enterprises do not emerge automatically instead, they are socially constructed "by individuals whose action is both facilitated and constrained by the structure and resources available" (1992, p. 7). Hence, the indeterminacy and highly problematic nature of governmentality in service provision are practical accomplishments but in their very social construction are contingent upon many forms of contradictory actions and negotiated constraints. This article has attempted to unravel some vital theoretical debates into an understanding of the complex interrelationship between old age, professional power, and policy narratives. The use of a Foucauldian framework opens up the pathway for understanding social relations in the matrix relationship of identity, professionalism, and policy – a vital contribution to unpacking the life course.

Chapter 4

AGING, FOUCAULT AND THE LIFE COURSE

INTRODUCTION

Recently, there has been an unprecedented international rise in interest and debate about aging, life course and social work (Leonard, 1997). This paper draws upon the theoretical work of Michel Foucault in order to sketch out a possible "tool-kit" for the critical analysis of social work as it has been characterized in social discourse. More specifically, we suggest that Foucault's ideas can be used to understand the construction of social welfare. This paper attempts an initial assessment of the relevance of Foucauldian analyses and offers novel insights about the changing influence of social welfare.

Over the past 20 years, modern social work in the United Kingdom, like elsewhere in Canada, Australia and North America has experienced an intense process of rationalization. Social work is essentially a political activity (Gregory and Holloway, 2005), constantly having to respond to challenges that reflect dynamics produced by the shifting priorities of government (Gilbert and Powell, 2005). In the UK, most pressing have been concerns identified with the degeneration of the social democratic accord implied by the *'post war settlement'* (Clarke and Newman, 1997; Harris, 2002), as it gave way to new priorities produced by the neo-liberal consensus that emerged since the 1980s. This has seen 'New Labour' governments extend the project of restructuring the relationship between the state and its citizens initiated by New Right Conservatives (Jordan, 2005). Social services, once envisaged as the province of a universal citizenship are now mere supports for the irresponsible (Butler and Drakeford, 2001; Harris, 2002). Despite this, there has been very little Foucauldian analysis of social work and its relationship to power. This leads us to argue that a Foucauldian analysis of power relations needs to explore the forms of governmentality that regulate and manage the everyday lives of citizens. The state, once the principle focus for analysis, now appears as merely one among a range of contextually and historically specific elements within multiple circuits of power (Rose, 1999). Therefore, we need to identify the assemblage of ruling practices, knowledge authorities and moral imperatives, which converge on social work in order to govern the conduct of social workers and those they aim to support (Rose and Miller, 1992; Parton, 1994; Rose, 1996; 1999). In this formulation, differences between the government of populations and management of conduct in specific localized spaces are technical rather than ontological. Social policy, enacted via a range of institutions [schools, universities, hospitals, workplaces] aims to act on the 'well-being' of the population as a whole promoting social cohesion while simultaneously acting on the innumerable decisions taken by individuals in their everyday lives thus managing their conduct (Rose, 1999).

To this end, we will first explore Foucault's ideas in relation to power and the concept of 'governmentality'. Following which we consider the changing context of contemporary social work and then move on to an application of Foucault's ideas to professional practice focusing on two areas: surveillance and social work and discretion and power.

THE POWER OF MICHEL FOUCAULT

Most of Michel Foucault's theoretical schemas are posed in oppositional terms. He urges individuals to "refuse what we are" (1982: 216), meaning that we should refuse to remain tied to fixed identities to which people are subjected. He linked his own project with all those who struggle against the ways in which they are individualized, particularized, and objectified by controlling discourses. It is important, at this stage, to map out a number of key Foucauldian concepts that will later be used to address the relationship between identity and changing welfare policies. These key concepts include: genealogy and discourse, power/knowledge, and technologies of self. The point of Foucault's analysis, called a genealogy because of its emphasis on tracing historical pathways that have contributed to contemporary circumstances, was to identify discourses. His concept of "discourse" is a key term both in understanding Foucault's work and in explaining facets of social welfare. Foucault identified discourses as historically variable ways of specifying knowledge and truth. function as sets of rules, and the exercise of these rules and discourses in programs that specify what is or is not the case–what constitutes "old age," for example. Those who are labeled "old" are in the grip of power. This power would include that operated by professional social workers through institutions and face-to-face interactions with their patients and clients. Power is constituted in discourses, and it is in discourses such as those of "social work" that power lies. Genealogy is concerned, then, with the historical limits and conditions of socially determined discourses, which then direct and distort the personal and institutional narratives that can subsist within them. When a discourse has stabilized historically, it can be referred to as a "discursive formation," which can come to characterize a particular period of welfare development and the associated possibilities for identity performance that it contains. Foucault (1967) was particularly interested in the limits and possibilities of discourses from "human sciences" because of their attempts to define human subjectivity. His attention shifts to the power of professionals because Foucault found that the conditions of possibility for "true" discourses about human subjects include complex relations between knowledge about people and systems of power. Here Foucault focuses on the techniques of power/knowledge that operate within an institution and that simultaneously create "a whole domain of knowledge and a whole type of power" (1977, p. 185).

These domains effectively destroy the legitimacy of other, competing, discourses; just as a professional medical opinion might de-legitimize voices arising from folk medicine or informal care. The genealogical work of uncloaking these power relations is characterized, by Foucault, as setting out the "political regime of the production of truth" (Davidson, 1986, p. 224). The effects of the reflexive relationship between power and knowledge that is implied here would include the tendency for professional power to be reinforced by the sorts of questions professionals ask and the data they collect. This knowledge then progresses to a certain definition of a problem area that then feeds back to stabilize the original formulation of the "problem" itself. By the same token, different policy positions point professionals to seek out certain forms of knowledge that tend to reinforce the ideological position of that policy and its associated discourses.

As part of this process, certain powerful voices increase their legitimacy, while other, often dissenting, voices become de-legitimized. An effect of the mutually reinforcing relationship between power and knowledge that emerges from the above is to construct individuals simultaneously as subjects and as objects. First, people are seen as objects by someone else, through control and restraint. Second, people are deemed to actively subject their own identity to personal direction through processes such as conscience and mediated self-knowledge. Foucault (1988) refers to this second process as "technologies of self." Foucault's formulation of "technologies of self" claims that individual lives are never quite complete and finished–that in order to function socially individuals must somehow work on themselves to turn themselves into subjects. The notion of "technologies" offers the scope for an analysis of the sites whereby certain effects on old age are brought about. As Foucault puts it: "Both meanings [of control and self-conscience] suggest a form of power which subjugates and makes subject to" (1982, p. 212).

In terms of social welfare, itself a discourse, both clients and social workers would need not simply to follow the rules that legitimize what they can say and do, but also to work on themselves so each can become the sort of person who can be seen and heard within that discourse. If they are not careful, both professionals and users of health and welfare systems become trapped in a dance of mutually maintained positions that serves to sustain a particular view of the world and the remedies, the technologies, that can be brought to bear on it. An analysis of power, which follows the Foucauldian pathway as it is outlined above, must examine at least three aspects of how such power is created and maintained. First, the analysis must examine the genealogy of existing relations, how they have emerged, and the discourses they both reflect and reinforce with respect to aging. Second, attention must be given to the distribution of power and knowledge that these relations imply. Finally, technologies of welfare such as psycho-casework and case management will need to be critically assessed as approaches to the self that hold certain webs of power in place. Each will contribute to the ways in which subjects enmeshed in certain relations apply techniques of identity control to themselves.

For Foucault (1977) power is a concept often discussed as fundamental to the relationship between professionals and the society in which they operate but one rarely conceptualized as both product and producer of such relationships. For example, Michel Foucault's analysis of power offers a set of strategies (Foucault, 1977; 1978) for understanding how discourse produced within a network of disciplinary activities and embedded in social policy constructs social workers' experiences and their identities, as well as the experiences and identities of those with whom they interact. At the same time, the dynamics of these relationships reinforce and modify the discourse that made such meaning possible in the first place.

Bryan Turner (1997) argues that Foucault's contribution to the analysis of power is important in three ways as it provides: (a) analysis of the relationship between power and knowledge; (b) the emergence of the modern self through disciplinary technologies and; (c) analysis of governmentality. Central to Foucauldian analysis is discourse, inseparable combinations of knowledge and power that along with their respective technologies [specific techniques and associated practices, i.e., assessment, care planning] operate to subjugate individuals in specific circulations or 'regimes of power'.

Foucault proposes that since the seventeenth century a particularly modern form of power has developed; 'bio-politics', a politics of the population that operates through two modalities, 'totalizing' and 'individualizing', producing a two-way process between the subject as a private individual and the subject as a public citizen (Miller, 1993). Foucault rejects claims that any particular group or class have a monopoly over power rather, power circulates via a myriad of social networks penetrating deep into the far corners of social life playing out its effects through the everyday interactions of autonomous individuals. Power and knowledge combine in disciplinary processes that act on the body producing the modern subject as docile, productive and willing to participate in their own management (Foucault, 1977). Through these processes, power operates to differentiate groups of people and individuals from other individuals, finally producing the components of individual subjectivity.

Foucault uses the idea of 'resistance' to describe how the effects of power may be only partially successful in specific social contexts enabling challenges to and changes in existing power relations (Nettleton 1997). This occurs in a number of ways but is located with two forms of possibility. First, the re-emergence of 'popular knowledges', the historical contents of conflict and struggle that have become submerged under a veneer of functionalist coherence and order; and second 'insurrections of subjugated knowledges', knowledges disqualified as inadequate, unscientific or lacking sophistication. In both these possibilities, we can see the possibility of a range of accounts, i.e., professionals alienated from practice, oppressed communities, and the disadvantaged and disenfranchised.

In this formulation, Foucault (1977) departs from many conceptualizations of power by suggesting that power in itself is 'relational' (Parton, 1994). Therefore, whilst one social actor may exercise power interacting with other individuals, we also need to be aware that all other individuals also exercise 'power' in their social relationships often expressed through 'resistance' in its dance with surveillance. The outcome is to produce a dialectical relationship between knowledge, power and action that is productive in the sense of creating particular possibilities but which also maintains a level of uncertainty and unpredictability in terms of actions, providing opportunity for the exercise of discretion.

In relation to the modern self, Foucault (1977) identifies three key processes in the objectification of individuals. Hierarchical observation, the development of ever-sophisticated processes of surveillance (often discussed as 'panopticon' or the 'gaze') that are constantly but unobtrusively maintained engulfing all in a web of watching. Normalising judgements, the production of classification systems that enable the identification of 'norms' of social functioning that allow ongoing comparison of individuals enabling small transgressions to become the focus of disciplinary attention and; the examination. The latter brings together the two former elements linking specific knowledges with particular practices in the exercise of power while engaging experts [professionals] in a network of writing and documentary accumulation that identifies individuals as deserving or risky, noting individual features, specifying appropriate interventions and recording progress. Documentation fixes the objectification of individuals in writing codifying, calculating difference and drawing comparison and embedding this in discourse, i.e., 'evidence based practice' which, in turn, disciplines and regulates professional activity.

However, rather than the objectifying processes discussed above, Foucault's (1977) concept of 'subjectification' involves a range of 'technologies of the self' where individuals engage with processes Foucault likens to the confessional. Individuals, incited by discourse, engage in reflective processes where they speak the truth about themselves, gain self-knowledge, and then act on that self-knowledge in an ethic of self-formation producing the self-managing individual central to neo-liberal rule (Dreyfus and Rabinow, 1982; Turner, 1997; Miller, 1993).

Analysis of Governmentality focuses on the processes, techniques and procedures that produce the moral regulation of the choices of autonomous individuals (Miller, 1993; Rose, 1993; 1996; Osborne, 1997); a feature of the very core of contemporary social policy thus enabling us to identify ways in which discourse constitutes categories of identity, regulating morals and directing life choices. Such processes of ethical self-formation give rise to a core feature of neo-liberal forms of government, the government of the self by the self. Discourse operates through a myriad of social institutions both statutory and non-statutory such as, citizen associations, charities, trade unions, families, schools, hospitals, workplaces that have no direct political affiliations and diverse histories.

Finally, Foucault's (1978) conceptual tool of 'governmentality' is the means through which neo-liberal modes of government afford expertise a key role and function in the management of both individual and collective conduct. However, this role differs markedly from that afforded professionals under former regimes as neo-liberal government: 'seeks to detach the substantive authority of expertise from the apparatus of political rule, relocating experts within a market governed by the rationalities of competition, accountability and consumer demand' (Rose 1993: 285). Government, rather than being the territory of direct interventions, becomes instead the structuring and regulation of potential choices of autonomous individuals with expertise operating in a semi-autonomous relationship with the state (Miller 1993). This has had an impact on the professional changes in social work.

MODERN SOCIAL WORK IN ENGLAND

Over the past 5 years, new policy frameworks have emerged in England covering both children and adults, *Every Child Matters* (DH, 2003), *Independence, Well Being and Choice* (DH, 2005a), *Choosing Health* (DH, 2005b) *Our Health, Our Care, Our Say* (DH, 2006*)* and *Putting People First (HM Government 2007),* profoundly restructuring the terrain of social work, social care, education and health. At the macro-level, this framework [bio-politics] targets the population with notions of 'Well Being' articulated with discourses of social inclusion and responsibility. At the micro-level its effects work by managing individual conduct inciting individuals to seek 'well-being' by balancing choices between the often-contradictory imperatives of the 'market' with those of individual and collective obligation (Rose, 1999); this establishing the basis for moral self-regulation mirrored in a myriad of formal and informal social contexts (Miller, 1993).

This formula is not merely rhetorical. Organisational structures across a range of social institutions including personal social services reflect similar logic. The introduction of quasi-markets in social services separated functions previously held within unified departments dividing assessment of need from the provision of support; the latter devolved to an increasing range of semi-autonomous organizations in the third sector (Clarke and Newman 1997). In conjunction, government acts indirectly on these autonomous organizations identifying budgets, setting targets and regulating activity while individual organizations act reflexively and demonstrate effective self-management (Rose, 1999). As part of this, the role of social workers are shaped by increasing managerialist demands for information particularly in response to audit and risk assessment (Parrot and Madoc-Jones, 2008) leading to claims of increased paperwork with a corresponding demise of face-to-face work (Sheppard, 1995; Lewis and Glennerster, 1996; Pithouse, 1998; Jones, 2001; Postle, 2001).

This new policy framework added another dimension to the increasingly dispersed context of social care by effectively dividing provision for children and families from provision for adults. This has been added to more recently by demands for specialisation in pre-qualifying social work training (Laming, 2009); the former leaving some to comment that developments represent the final nail in the coffin of the unified social work department envisaged by Seebohm (Garrett, 2002). In addition, lead roles, once clearly the province of social services are now set within a complex array of relationships between statutory and non-statutory organizations, including a range of service user and other consumer groups. Such relations often reflect power relationships at a more local level, highlighting Foucault's emphasis on the importance of micro-politics (Gordon 1980) which, in the process, produce an increasingly diverse range of roles for social workers operating in the different segments of welfare. In addition, a whole plethora of new roles have emerged, e.g., personal advisors in Connexions service, which have chipped away at the traditional bases of the social work role. At the same time, information and communication technologies have provided a new novel spaces for organising meaning (Salvo, 2004), effectively structuring activities such as assessment, establishing modern opportunities for the surveillance of workers and service users (Garrett, 2002; 2005), while also providing innovative possibilities for representing the disadvantaged.

Notwithstanding clear differences in the power and prestige of so-called 'caring professions' (Hugman, 1991), traditional professions such as medicine, as well as newer and less established 'quasi-professions' such as social work, have been considered more resistant to, or even immune from, broader economic and political power. Reasons for this assumption have differed, but in general the professions reliance upon knowledge and technical skill for practice, as well as internally restricted access and an extensive period of academic training, have allowed employee discretion and control to prevail (Johnston, 1972). However, critics have challenged this orthodox view noting the extent to which professions have always tended to readily adapt to forces of change, as well as conform to externally dictated organisational policy and procedures (Brint, 1994; Johnson 2001). For example, the expansion of managerialism has significantly reduced prior discretions (Jones, 2001; Baines, 2004). Despite this, it is questionable the extent to which professional practice has been seriously challenged by resistance due to resurgence of popular or subjugated knowledges of service users (Chambon, 1999).

Hence, a Foucauldian approach to social work professions (Biggs and Powell, 2001; Fournier, 1999; 2000; 2001) attempts to integrate the micro-political tactics of professionalisation within a broader network of power relations through the analysis of discourse and regimes of power/knowledge. For Foucault, professionalism is in itself 'a disciplinary mechanism'; associating specific practices with particular worker identities, knowledge and rules of conduct thus legitimising professional authority and activity. In turn, these norms act as a form of *discipline* over otherwise autonomous professional power regulating behaviour through self-management (Fournier, 1999). Thus induction into professions, in terms of *both* knowledge *and* conduct, serves to construct a specifically governable subjectivity rooted in self-disciplinary mechanisms such as reflective practice and models of supervision (Grey, 1998; Gilbert, 2001). Therefore, the political proximity of welfare professions to the apparatus of government can be described as follows: 'professionals are both the instrument and the subject of government, the governor and the governed' (Fournier, 1999: 285).

Paradoxically, professional autonomy, particularly in areas such as social work, is both the reason why the professions remain necessary, due to their ability to manage complex and unpredictable situations, and the focus for the deployment of a range of disciplinary technologies that produce patterns of accountability that target, limit and control the exercise of autonomy (Rose, 1999). Indeed, Biggs and Powell (2001: 99) warn:

> In terms of social welfare, itself a discourse, both clients and social workers would need not simply to follow the rules that legitimise what they can say and do, but also to work on themselves in order to become the sort of person who can be seen and heard within that discourse. If they are not careful, both professionals and users of health and welfare systems become trapped in a dance of mutually maintained positions that serves to sustain a particular view of the world and the remedies, the technologies, that can be brought to bear on it.

This view of welfare professions as modes of disciplinary control also provides a useful counterbalance to critical perspectives, which reinforce stereotypes of pampered and privileged professionalism. In recasting professionalism as a source of influence and status concomitant with self-discipline and controlled performance, the Foucauldian position also links professionals with a wider range of control strategies (Dyer and Keller-Cohen, 2000; Fleming, 2005; Hochschild, 1983; Whitehead, 1998). This places professional expertise at the heart of disciplinary technologies designed for the management of populations.

SOCIAL WORK AND SURVEILLANCE

In this next section, we aim to extend this Foucauldian analysis by focusing on two contemporary issues faced by social work practitioners both of which involve different technologies of surveillance.

The first concerns systems of knowledge provided by information and communications technologies [ICT], which shape social work activity while the second considers that archetypal proviso for professional autonomy, the exercise of discretion. Together these two pillars of contemporary practice demonstrate all three elements of what Foucault (1977) describes as discipline: hierarchical observation, normalizing judgments and the examination. For example, the clients of social work practice as well as social workers' themselves as both object and subject subjugating both to ever more-sophisticated modes of surveillance while paradoxically creating spaces for innovation and resistance. In the case of the former, we explore the objectifying effect of audit and the way this exploits electronic capabilities for surveillance (Garrett, 2005; Rose, 1999), while the latter retains the familiar professional technologies of supervision promoting self-reflexive surveillance (Rose, 1996; 1999; Gilbert, 2001).

Indeed, one of the key issues in health and social care, where a Foucauldian approach illuminates its microphysics of power can be situated within an exemplar of information and communication technologies. Salvo (2004:43) describes 'communication and information systems' as the art, science and business of organizing information so that it makes sense to people who use it while also highlighting its' democratizing potential theoretically promoted by participation. However, in practice, *Data Protection and Freedom of Information legislation* circumscribe these technologies promoting a potentially contradictory position that both enables and restricts access to information. In UK health and social services, this tension demands adherence to the 'Caldicott standard' (DH, 2002; Richardson and Asthana, 2006). Salvo also highlights the potential of such technologies as 'professional space' promoting what he describes as 'critical action' which also opens up the possibility of both innovation and resistance as workers exploit the totalizing effects of such processes. Similarly, Parrot and Madoc-Jones explore the potential of ICT for resistance, the exercise of discretion and the development of new forms of social work practice.

Nevertheless, information and communications technologies increasingly order the practice of a range of professionals including social workers subsuming in the process older paper-based standardized assessment and associated needs focused processes. Garrett (2002; 2005) notes the pervasiveness of such technologies across the public sector, thus ensuring that it is impossible to avoid engaging with these technologies at some level. The implication being that adopting a stance of 'refusing to participate' is not a serious option (Freenberg, 1991) although, resistance and subversion are always possibilities (Fleming, 2005).

Information and communication technology is a core element of policy and central to strategies for governing social welfare often located within the rhetoric of 'joined up government' and influenced by the private sector (Garrett, 2005; Hudson, 2000a; b; Selwyn, 2002). Parallel rhetoric of 'shared assessment processes' recruit both the service user and a range of professionals in both statutory and non-statutory agencies to 'data sharing' supported by such technologies. At the same time, a variety of management information systems enable the passing of performance data between localized and centralized levels of government linking the two poles of bio-politics.

The significance of these systems from a Foucauldian perspective is twofold. First, they engulf all in architectural labyrinth of information, a form of panopticon establishing a level of surveillance of both worker and service user, constantly monitored through electronic forms of audit. Second, they institutionalize particular discourses in the very operation of the system through the nature and types of questions asked. Garrett (2005: 453) notes the *'narrow, normative and prescriptive view'* embedded in a range of assessment tools promoted by government agencies observing that:

> ... Social work is increasingly being ordered, devised and structured by academics, policy makers and e-technicians far removed from the day-to-day encounters, which practitioners have with the users of services. This is reflected in the emerging software architecture and in the greater use of centrally devised e-assessment templates which attempt to map contours of social work engagements and which construct new 'workflows'. (Garrett 2005: 545)

In England, guidelines related to community care policy (DHSS, 1990; DH, 2005b; 2006) provide familiar strategies of identification, assessment, care planning, care packages, monitoring and review. However, subtle changes in the rationalized deployment of this technology shifted its focus away from support for clients and toward surveillance and monitoring. A new language of audit concerned with 'outcomes' and 'risk' shaped social work activity both in child care and community care producing particular expectations (Rose, 1999; D'Cruz et al., 2009). Monroe (2004) notes both positive and negative consequences of this development but in a similar vein to Garrett (2005), observes the involvement of external inspectorates such as the Audit Commission and the Social Services Inspectorate alongside senior managers in setting goals and an absence of practicing social workers. Positive developments include increased accountability and standardization of social work practice however; this may be at the cost of producing a punitive environment and reducing social work to a simplistic description of practice that operates within a culture of blame and protocolisation.

Furthermore, in the context of child welfare, Tilbury (2004) notes how the values implicit in performance indicators provide a narrow conception of child welfare that overstates regulatory concerns while underplaying the importance of supporting families to provide safe care at home. Likewise, Garrett (2003:443) observes that the 'Framework for Assessment of Children in Need and their Families (DH/DfEE/HO, 2000), contains a preoccupation with the ecological approach and the use of questionnaires and scales that produces social work as a reactive activity narrowly focused on child abuse at the expense of proactive family support services.

This 'narrow, normative and prescriptive view' has particular consequences for some targets of policy due to what Booth et al. (2006) describe as 'temporal discrimination'. Discussing the experience of child protection procedures by parents with intellectual disabilities they note how the prevailing wisdom in policy and practice over avoiding delays and the tendency for time-limited interventions works against people with poor conceptions of time and related skills. They argue that 'tick box' social work reliant on systems and procedures has replaced analysis and judgment to the detriment of some of the most vulnerable of social workers' clients. This provides a new tactic for the surveillance of contemporary social work that can best be described as 'time discipline' (Garrett, 2003), reflecting Jones' (2001) observation that tactics first used to constrain the autonomy of radical social workers now targets mainstream practitioners. Processes of protocolization, the time spent on activities such as paperwork [or electronic form filling] has particular relevance for a Foucauldian analysis of social work, as power relations embedded in routinization can 'define a certain pattern of 'normalization':

> The carceral network, in its compact or disseminated forms, with its systems of insertion, distribution, surveillance, observation, has been the greatest support, in modern society, of the normalizing power. (Foucault 1977: 304)

Keenan (2001) observes similar phenomena in the USA related to compulsory documentation and recording for users of mental health services. She describes the constricted, objectifying image of service users provided by the assessment and monitoring processes informed by the normalizing and medicalized discourses of mental health embedded in *The Diagnostic and Statistical Manual of Mental Disorders* (DSM IVR, 1994), which define healthy behaviours in relation to particular norms and in opposition to unhealthy or forbidden behaviours. At the same time, she uses Foucauldian insights to identify how the 'gaze' of diagnosis makes the service user visible while shading the powerful and privileged.

In a similar vein, Scheyett (2006) argues that discourses of evidence based practice effectively silence both the service user and the practitioner. This occurs as the dialogue between service users and practitioners over experiences and knowledge of the 'real world' become subjugated to disciplinary knowledge external to this dialogue which, through its status as truth, discredits alternative conceptions of events and their meanings (Foucault, 1978). As tactics of government, information technologies objectify and render visible but in the same movement silence the targets of policy. As Heffernan (2006) notes, the language of user involvement dispersed throughout social policy, has enabled government to narrow the range of options available.

Social work clients are not the only targets of the discourses carried by this information infrastructure. The rights of carers to have their needs assessed has valorized both caring and carers in a way that 'may squeeze out the last remnants of the right not to care' thus reinforcing a particular ethical gaze within objectified and electronic formats (Harris, 2002). Greater visibility of carers is a consequence of their increasing status within tactics of government that have also brought greater levels of surveillance (Heaton, 1999; Henderson and Forbat, 2002) cementing forms of obligation distilled from this 'ethic' of care. Together these shifts contribute to the downgrading of holistic and ethical practice (Gregory and Holloway, 2005).

Foucault (1977) views surveillance as a central technique that renders an individual the object of power/knowledge. Assessment practice, established in relation to normalized standards and roles as in this example, produces an intensification of paperwork, protocolization and the expansion of information and communication technologies. Hence, professionals also come under scrutiny as part of the continuous review of the client's needs. A gaze that is 'always receptive' to managerial control catches all (Foucault 1977: 89).

SOCIAL WORK, POWER AND DISCRETION

The exercise of discretion, taken as the archetypal activity that defines professional practice, has provided the focus for a significant amount of debate and analysis concerning the status of professions in general and social work in particular. Discretion provides a paradoxical space for the operation of power both enticing resistance and inviting surveillance. The majority of this debate has focused on the way managerialism, managerial forms of supervision and information technology has apparently undermined professional discretion (Harris, 1998; Evans and Harris, 2004; D'Cruz et al., 2009). Nevertheless, Evans and Harris (2004), provide an interesting discussion of discretion in social work practice drawing on Lipsky's (1980) work on 'street level bureaucracies' which focused on face-to-face encounters of social workers with their clients. Analysis provides evidence that discretion is alive and well in social work practice although micro-politics of the context means that this has been subject to ongoing revision: again the dance of resistance and surveillance.

The spaces within which social workers 'translate nebulous policy into practical action' (Evans and Harris, 2004: 882) resonate with the analysis of governmentality and the persistence of professional authority in complex situations where actions cannot be pre-prescribed. Persistence of spaces between rules requires judgments by professionals over which 'rules' apply in contexts that contain multiple possibilities. Practitioners also use discretion when deciding to 'apply the rules' in this instance effectively closing down space. This leads to the proposition that discretion is a political activity that occurs in the context of uncertainty and complexity necessitating negotiation while highlighting localized and relational aspects of power.

This localized and relational aspect is also evident in power relations between practitioners and managers where enabling discretion has advantages for managers and organizations as it allows 'innovation' to be claimed for the organization when things work well while directing blame at front line practitioners when things go wrong, i.e., 'failed to follow procedures'. In addition, discretion allows managers to distance themselves from difficult day-to-day consequences of organizational goals such as gaps between actions and resources. Discretion therefore operates in spaces governed by uncertainty that involve bargaining and negotiation over responsibility (Evans and Harris, 2004). Indeed, networks of power relations operating via the most mundane interactions between managers, social workers, service users and carers enable the formation and shifting of alliances between political and non-political authorities where experts [professionals] and expertise are crucial to operations (Parton, 1994; D'Cruz, et al., 2009). 'Micro-politics' is the localized context where policy decisions are given meaning through practical application and the identities of participants are produced in the reciprocal relations of power or 'performativity'. Performance is always relational, drawing others into the act: managers, other professionals, clients and so on constructing both meanings associated with performances and mutually dependent subject positions (Wetherell, 2001).

Such specific and localized contexts are typically complex with multiple demands providing circumstances where social workers can adopt different roles depending on their function and client group. There is always some degree of fluidity and uncertainty around expectations and therefore the space for discretion and thus innovation and resistance. In addition, social workers carry a range of discourses into these spaces. Face-to-face contact enables different forms of interaction from that characterized in routinized and objectified practice. It also allows social workers to 'reclaim the language' to re-establish holistic and ethical practice:

> Deconstructing the language of performance indicators and quality outcomes implies that rather than turning a conversation with a service user about how they think and feel about their situation into easily measurable service inputs, the social worker strives to reflect that conversation in the framing of objectives driven by the service user's internalized understanding of 'quality'. (Gregory and Holloway 2005: 50)

However, it is not sufficient to assume that all face-to-face encounters are in themselves holistic and ethical and by that alone avoid the oppressive nature of objectifying discourses and routinized practice. For example, discourses of anti-oppressive practice developed from a radical critique of social work causing the profession to reflect and review practice with major benefits at that time however; this discourse is now the nucleus of social work activity. Language and meaning associated with anti-racist and anti-oppressive practice are historically specific while discourse is dynamic allowing re-articulation of radical elements with more conservative positions that colonize and neutralize the discourse institutionalizing it in a range of organizational contexts:

> Indeed anti-oppressive practice has allowed the state to reposition itself as a benign arbiter between competing identity claims. Perversely, given its aim to make the personal political, it has allowed the problems of society to be recast as due to the moral failings of individuals who need censure and correction from the anti-oppressive social worker. (McLaughlin, 2005: 300)

Similar contradictions arise in relation to the discourse of 'empowerment', which has become a theory of professional practice providing professionals with a central role in defining needs and designing interventions (Pease, 2002). Rose (1996), takes this criticism a stage further suggesting that discourses of empowerment translate as the 'role of experts in the coaxing of others who lack the cognitive, emotional, practical and ethical skills to take personal responsibility and engage in self-management'. Disciplinary techniques embedded in discourses of empowerment located in initiatives such as 'Sure Start' (DH, 2003), 'community development projects', and public health projects (DH, 2004), target 'damaged individuals' in an attempt to reform and normalize their conduct, encouraging them to take personal responsibility and engage in self-forming activities, self-care and self-help (Rose, 1999; Jordan, 2000).

Nevertheless, a number of writers (Beresford, 2001; Butler, 2005; Harris, 1998; Evans and Harris, 2004; Gregory and Holloway, 2005; Hodge, 2005; Scheyett, 2006; Pease, 2002) emphasize, in different ways, social workers' potential for resistance in their practice with marginalized individuals and groups. Under such circumstances social workers resist prevailing discourse defining individuals, i.e., refugees and asylum seekers as a problem and undeserving. Instead, they provide space for the service users' to develop and express their perspective on needs and priorities. Here, discretion provides space for the renegotiation of events making resistance possible through the 'insurrection of subjugated knowledges'.

However, such possibilities may already be constrained regardless of the values of individual social workers. Social workers' carry into their interactions 'icons' representing the collective experience of society concerning particular types of event (Kitzinger, 2000). These 'icons' are produced over time as a consequence of similar types of events, e.g., child abuse cases, homicides perpetrated by users of mental health services, neglect and deaths of people subject to community care. Such events provoke intense media discussion while icons provide rhetorical shorthand for journalists and the public, which include interpretive frameworks that embed distortion and inaccuracy and provide templates for future events. As such, they have particular qualities; appear fixed and authoritative, and resist renegotiation. Discursively, they provide a backdrop for social work activity disciplining discretion through ghost-like media surveillance.

Surveillance in this world of face-to-face encounters takes more subtle forms than those produced by objectifying processes of routinized work, and information and communication technologies. Nevertheless, the dual aspect of bio-politics remains evident. At the macro-level, governance of professional activity requires professions to regulate the activity of practitioners by ensuring their commitment to professional development as a prerequisite to retaining a license to practice. At the micro-level, discourse concerning the complexity of the social work task incites individual practitioners to adopt a position of reflexivity to their work (Taylor and White, 2000). Such reflexivity, achieved via confessional practices includes, among others, techniques of reflection and supervision (Rose, 1999; Gilbert, 2001). In turn, organizations require practitioners to engage in supervision as surveillance of individual practice; thus promoting processes that enable managers to maintain 'the gaze' on both individual social workers and the exercise of discretion in relation to their caseload. Managers themselves are also subject to supervision entangling all in an ever-extending web of surveillance.

Such subjectifying technologies operating alongside the objectifying technologies discussed earlier, exemplified by the use of information and communication technologies, reproduce the panopticon in a contemporary form no longer constrained by the physical limits of the hospital, school, prison or barracks; enabling the surveillance of social work activity across an increasingly complex and dispersed landscape. For Foucault (1977), the panopticon integrates power and knowledge, the control of the 'body' and the control of space into a technology of discipline. To this, as noted earlier, we can also add a temporal dimension. It is both efficient, since surveillance is everywhere and constant, and effective, because it is 'discreet', functioning 'permanently and in silence' (1977: 177). It also provides the scope for the supervision of those entrusted with the surveillance of others.

CONCLUSION

The advancing of the neo-liberal project initiated by New Right Conservatives and extended by New Labour has seen a radical restructuring of the terrain of welfare. In parallel with these changes, new relations of power and knowledge emerge providing different forms of oppression and different possibilities for those reliant on welfare services. Adopting a Foucauldian approach enables a critical approach to the dynamics of knowledge and power that lays open the implications and the possibilities of practices promoted by social policy and enacted by social workers. In addition, this perspective, by moving beyond conceptions of power as domination to consider power as relational poses a different range of questions over how particular subjects are formed, e.g., asylum seekers. Moreover, it raises questions over how that identity relates to the formation of other subjects on which subjectivity is dependent.

Furthermore, exploring power as relational exposes many of the principles that have guided social work activity such as empowerment and anti-oppressive to a critical stance, identifying how relations of power have seen such commitments detached from their original radical and humanitarian moorings to feature now as components of oppressive discourses they might once have challenged. Nevertheless, by identifying the effects of power as partial a Foucauldian perspective provides the possibility of resistance enabling analysis of those many incidences, many mundane, some striking, where service users may come together with carers and social workers to establish alternatives to prevailing discourse and social practices. To contribute to this possibility social work is in need a of Foucauldian theory of power relations. Clarification takes place through an examination of the presuppositions that are embedded in world-views of social workers. However, these developments in social work have their shadow side, and the ethics of using such technologies to "help" clients such as older people through complex power relations have been subject to less scrutiny.

Chapter 5

TRUST, THE LIFE COURSE AND SOCIAL RELATIONS

Trust receives a great deal of pubic exposure grounded in the assumption that the level of trust placed by the public in particular people, offices, professions, institutions or systems is critical to its continuing authority. There are increasing attempts to conceptualize the notion of 'trust' in social theory as a pivotal dimension of modernity (Powell 2014). Trust, either personal or impersonal (Misztal 1996), can be viewed as fundamental to inter-personal informal relationships (Brownlie and Howson 2005), to the working of organizations (Morgan 2002), and to professionals (Gilbert 2001) - all fundamentally linked to the occidental world of modernity (Delanty 2005).

The early observation that 'social science research concerning trust has produced a good deal of conceptual confusion regarding the meaning of trust and its place in social life' continues to have relevance today (Lewis and Weigert 1985 quoted in Powell, 2005, 76). On the one hand incompatible with complete ignorance of the possibility and probability of future events, and on the other hand, with emphatic belief, which excludes the anticipation of disappointment. Trust has provided the essence for a range of contemporary debates within the social sciences although these have taken different foci. A deal of theorising has taken place against a backdrop of concerns over the weakening of community bonds and the challenges this holds for democratic institutions. In one conceptualization as 'social capital', trust can be seen as synthetic providing a form of glue or binding of individuals in communities (Phillipson, 2005) involved in a myriad of apparently independent social relationships (Giddens 1990, 1991, Putnam 1993, Fukuyama 1995, Misztal 1996, Lane 1998, Seligman 1997, Sztompka 1999, Uslaner 1999). In part, these discussions were provoked by and consequentially exposed the limitations of rational choice models and the post-emotionalism thesis as a means of explaining human behaviour (Taylor-Gooby and Zinn 2007; Dean 2007). 'Trust' itself is an essentially contested concept. Trust can extend to people with a sense of shared identity (Gilson 2003, Tulloch and Lupton 2003). Individuals produce trust through experience and over time. It cannot be immediately and with purpose be produced by organizations or governments without dialogical interaction with people on issues affecting their lifestyles and life-chances such as care, pensions, employment and political representation (Walker and Naeghele, 1999). Möllering (2001) takes the relational theme further by distinguishing between trust in contracts between individuals and the State in areas such as pension provision; trust in friendships across intergenerational lines; trust in love and relationships, and trust in foreign issues associated with national identity. There is a multiplicity of ways that trust has been defined but the central paradox is how to creation of the conditions of building conditions of trust across personal-organisational-structural tiers in an increasingly uncertain world.

Seligman's (1997) theorising of trust identifies important conceptual issues concerning the relationship between trust, confidence, faith and familiarity. Trust is unconditional while confidence enjoys more certainty than trust. We can have confidence in systems and roles but trust only in persons. Seligman suggests trust differs from faith, as unconditionally is secular and not related to deity while familiarity is a mechanism for maintaining confidence and ontological security.

Alternatively, Sztompka (1999) provides a model of a trust culture that has five conditions for trust: normative coherence; stability of social order; transparency of social organisation; familiarity of social environment and accountability of professionals and institutions. His model gives a lot to tradition in the production and maintenance of trust. In addition, he suggests that social stability is compatible with social change so long as change is gradual, regular, predictable and consistent. Discontinuous change and the fragmentation of tradition forms of authority result in a parallel disintegration of trust. Conditions all too familiar as characteristics of post-modern society (Rose 1996, 1999) leading to the conclusion implicit in Sztompka's own discussion that this model is incapable of explaining trust in post-modern society underpinned by unpredictability.

We consider the implications of theorizing trust and suggest that it provides analytical and experiential insight into the dynamics of health and social care professional relationships in contemporary society. We caution that in order to full embed 'trust' in theoretical analysis we need a 'way forward' (Sibeon 2004) that synthesises discussions of trust with the conditions set by governmentality analysis. We suggest that Michel Foucault's (1978) concept of 'governmentality' enables the exploration of the relationship between different conceptions of trust, the mechanisms for managing populations and the production of self-managing professionals who are, in this sense, trusting. According to Foucault governmentality comprises three tiers: it is the result of transformations within the modern state; it is a tendency to institutionalize a particular form of power, and it is the "ensemble formed by institutions, procedures, analyses and reflections. . . calculations and tactics" (pp. 102-3) that enable the exercise of power directed towards the regulation of a population using various apparatuses of expertise. Indeed, we aim to demonstrate the deployment of particular rationalities supporting trust and trust-based relationships as tactics of government. For without trust, activities reliant on co-operation between families and communities with future orientated expectations have no satisfactory basis on which they might be established.

By drawing out the cost and benefits of trust-based relationships, identifying the way the facework of experts maintain the legitimacy of systems and promotion social cohesion, is part of the process of constructing professional authority. Whilst it is analytically audacious to articulate trust with governmentality in the light of professional expertise in health and social care, it provides an important reference point that raises rich conceptual questions about nature and meanings of attachment related to trust. We begin the next section by attempting to highlight the levels of trust that impinges on social relationships at: individual, community, organisational and systemic levels.

NAVIGATING THE CONCEPTUAL COMPLEXITY OF TRUST

Trust: Individuals, Organisations, Community and Systems

The first key focus for theorising trust has been the interpersonal qualities of the individuals involved. Sztompka (1999) challenges theorists who consider interpersonal forms of trust as the primary form based on face-to-face encounters while subordinating all other forms of trust, collectively referred to as social trust. Rejecting any differentiation between interpersonal trust and social forms of trust, he proposes that the ever-increasing impersonal nature of relationships in systems is underpinned by our experiences of trust in face-to-face relations. This reliance on the interpersonal aspect of trust suffers from similar problems to Giddens (1990) use of 'ontological security', a product of early childhood experiences, as a prerequisite for individuals being able to form trusting relationships. This conservative element leaves those without positive childhood experiences stuck in a psychoanalytic mire with no potential for trusting, or by implication being trustworthy, while also failing to offer any means of recovery. A number of theorists (Davies 1999, Giddens 1991, Mechanic 1998) note the expectations lay people have of experts or professionals while at the same time this interpersonal level provides the human aspect or 'facework' for more impersonal forms of trust. Expectations of professionals include the following: specific competencies, specialised areas of knowledge and skills, disinterestedness and disclosure. Of particular importance are communication skills and the ability to present complex information. Alongside, run role expectations that demand experts act ethically and with integrity as true agents of their clients, requiring them to put personal beliefs and interests aside and acting to maximise benefit and to do no harm. Creating specialized spaces reinforced by fiduciary norms arising from: the custody and discretion over property, the opportunity and possession of expertise and the access to information; regulates the power/knowledge relationship between expertise and laypersons (Giddens 1991, Shapiro 1987).

The second level of trust is at community level. Evidence exists of a positive correlation between levels of interpersonal trust and levels of social capital (Putman 1993, Rothstein 2000), leading in part to calls for increasing the levels of civility and community responsibility in everyday life. However, while theorists (Misztal 1996, Putman 1993, Taylor-Gooby 1999, 2000, Sztompka 1999, Rothstein 2000, Dean 2003) support the idea of social norms and values overriding rational models of human behaviour, they say little about how these norms and values become established. Rothstein claims that the link between interpersonal trust and social capital is weak, as are propositions about the direction of community relationships. Rejecting functionalist explanations linking norms to the established configurations of power, he proposes a theory of 'collective memories' creating social norms in communities as a strategic political process. The essential ingredient is the creation of conditions of community relationships built on common values.

The third key issue is on trust and organisational context. Challenges to the 'trustworthiness' in organisations, regardless of whether they are public or third sector organisations, can have profound effects on confidence in that system. Producing increased demands for regulation, information and transparency; that is, increasing the demands for distrust.

The fourth major area of concern for theorising trust has focused on the declining trust in both state mediated social systems such health and social care and the professions embedded therein (Davies 1999, Phillipson, 1998, Welsh and Pringle 2001). Conceived as impersonal or systems trust (Giddens 1990, 1991, Luhmann 1979) this form of trust is developed and maintained by embedding expertise in systems that do not require the personal knowledge of any individual by another. Such systems employ a range of techniques of distrust, i.e., audit processes, target setting and third party inspections to demonstrate trustworthiness (Gilbert 1998, 2005).

Implications of Trust in Health and Social Care

Part of the confusion concerning the different levels of trust rests, according to Möllering (2001), with the failure to distinguish between the functional properties of trust and the foundations of how trust is created in health and social care. The former are the outcomes of trust, i.e., expectations, concerning issues such as: order, co-operation, reducing complexity and social capital. While the latter concern the nature or bases of trust, which, due to the assumption that they are rational, become lost and therefore not explored. Moreover, individuals make decisions on partial knowledge, a mix of weak inductive knowledge and faith regarding the consequences of an action. Möllering suggests that in some circumstances relational aspects producing either confidence or reciprocity might support decision-making. However, this knowledge moves us close to confidence, which according to Seligman's (1997) is a different quality. Nevertheless, building on Möllering's theory, Brownlie and Howson (2005) argue that trust is relational and impossible to understand in isolation. Trust occurs as individuals extract the known factors while bracketing off or suspending the unknown factors to avoid confusing decisions with uncertainty.

Gilson (2003) takes up this relational aspect of trust and claims that relationship issues provide the main challenges for health services. Making the link between systems and social capital, she compares UK and US health systems. Concluding that the general acceptance by the UK population of the altruistic element of the UK health system stands in stark contrast with the distrust, which accompanies health care in the USA where there is a belief that the system is organised to maximize the benefits for the medical profession. Gilson argues that trust involves both cognitive and affective elements. The former relates to a risk calculation where the costs and benefits of an action are calculated alongside of the degree of uncertainty derived from the dependency on the actions and intentions of another while the latter is linked to the generation of emotional bonds and obligations. Altruism provides a special case of trust where trusting and trustworthiness promote the social status of those involved in giving. Consequences for those dependent on giving remains a key question. For as Giddens (1990) notes trust is a very specific case of dependency: a dependency on expertise.

Providing circumstances that discredit the rationalities supporting governmental strategies, challenging expertise and consequently public trust is lost. In this sense we might consider the examples of; the Bristol Babies scandal (Davies 1999), the controversy around the MMR vaccine (Brownlie and Howson 2005); the pensions crisis (Lunt and Blundell 2000, Price and Ginn 2003), or more vividly, child safety and paedophilia (Bell 2002).

Other writers draw distinctions between trust and hope. Both Sztompka (1999) and Gilbert (1998, 2005) discuss trust and hope, with hope representing a situation of relative powerlessness, a situation exemplified by Gilbert who concludes that trust is a discourse of professionals and experts while hope is a user discourse.

Seligman argues that trust, conceived as it is in this debate, is unique to modernity. In traditional societies, trust has quite different bases. Moreover, sociological theories, which suppose a general change in modernity (cf. Beck, 1992, Giddens 1994), assume that with the erosion of traditional institutions and scientific knowledge trust becomes an issue more often produced actively by individuals than institutionally guaranteed. To resolve these tensions I propose Foucault's Governmentality thesis as the means to identify the role of trust, along with the mechanisms for the deployment of trust and the role of professional expertise. Social institutions such as health and social care disseminate a particular ethic of the self into the discrete corners of everyday lives of the population. Supported by a discursive framework promoting co-operative relations between people, communities and organisations this ethic is future orientated and promotes qualities and values that sustain trust-based relationships and forms of action. In the process of building co-operative relations, the role of professionals and professional authority is established. The next section carefully examines the conceptual possibilities for articulation of trust and governmentality.

Linking Professional Authority with Trust and Governmentality

Conceptually there are tensions but also interesting theoretical possibilities between late [high] modern and post-structuralist conceptions of society. Both identify the fragmentation of traditional forms of authority and expertise, and acknowledge the increasing complexity this produces through the availability of multiple sources of information and different lifestyle choices. As noted earlier late [high] modern conceptions of trust, acknowledge uncertainty and risk as the basis for necessitating trust and point to the failure of rational choice theories as evidence of the existence of social trust. Likewise, governmentality theorists, discuss risk and uncertainty at length (Rose 1996, 1999, Osborne 1997, Petersen 1997), but leave the discussion of [social] 'trust' to an observation that trust, traditionally placed in authority figures, has been replaced by audit (Rose 1999). The problem of creating co-operative relations between individuals and within groups and communities, both in the present and for the future, is left unresolved. Foucault's summary of the working of the state provides a useful starting point for this discussion:

> "it is the tactics of government which make possible the continual definition and redefinition of what is within the competence of the State and what is not, the public versus the private, and so on; thus the State can only be understood in its survival and its limits on the basis of the general tactics of governmentality." (Foucault 1979:21)

Our contention is that the 'governmentality thesis' as it has been developed by writers such as: Rose and Miller (1992), Burchell (1991), Rose (1996, 1999), Osborne (1997), Petersen (1997) holds the potential to overcome many of the problems experienced in theorising trust. It provides a means of extending the critical debate over trust. Linking discussions concerning the bases of trust: the conditions Möllering (2001) describes as essential for trust to happen with discussions focusing on the outcomes of trust, i.e., social capital, systems or impersonal trust and interpersonal trust

(Putnam 1993, Seligman 1997, Luhmann 1979, Giddens 1990, 1991, Sztompka 1999, Rothstein 2000).

Moreover, governmentality provides the means for identifying the mechanisms for deploying particular rationalities across the social fabric. In particular, the interplay between state intervention and the population that institutionalizes expertise as a conduit for the exercise of power in modern societies (Johnson 2001). Institutionalizing expertise establishes a range of specialized spaces: at once both hidden and visible, providing opportunities across the social landscape for a range of professionals. Experts who work on individuals inciting self-forming activity and individual agency, producing the self-managing citizen central to neo-liberal forms of government, 'enterprising subjects' or what Burchell (1991: 276) terms 'responsibilisation'. Thus enabling an explanation of trust that avoids resorting to a functionalist argument or an overly deterministic approach limited to either class action or the meaning-giving subject. Furthermore, governmentality can overcome the condition laid by Sztompka (1999) that trust cannot exist in conditions of discontinuous change. Indeed, in the context of discontinuous change, particular rationalities and their associated technologies become politicized, leading to increased conflict in the relationship between the state and expertise making trust an ever more valuable commodity.

In analysing the activities of government, Rose and Miller (1992: 175) argue, we must investigate 'political rationalities' and technologies of government - 'the complex of mundane programmes, calculations, techniques, apparatuses, documents and procedures through which authorities seek to embody and give effect to governmental ambitions'. In this case, rationalities, operating as discourses and social practices embodying a particular practical ethic, work to reproduce the norms, values and obligations associated with trust. Producing a subject position that values trustworthiness as both a personal characteristic and a characteristic sought in others. Both experts/professionals and the user/customer of health services emerge as the self-managing ethical subjects of neo-liberal rule (Miller 1993, Davidson 1994, Rose 1999).

For governmentality theorists an analysis of neo-liberal regimes reveals individuals as inculcated with values and objectives, orientated towards incorporating people as both players and partners in marketised systems including health and social care. Participation in markets along with the potential for unbounded choice are inextricably entwined with a creative tension, an ethical incompleteness, where private [selfish] desire and public [selfless] obligation produce the rational self-managing actor of neo-liberal rule. In a dialectical relationship that works to form individual identity through the exercise of a modern consumerist citizenship (Miller 1993). Such regimes exhort individuals; indeed expect them to become entrepreneurs in all spheres, and to accept responsibility for the management of 'risk'. Government is concerned with managing the conduct of conduct, the processes through which people 'govern' themselves, which includes an obligation to manage one's own health (Petersen 1997).

Theorists of modernity such as Putman (1993), Sztompka (1999) and Rothstein (2000) leave trust to arise organically through the interaction of individuals within groups and communities. The idea that increasing the levels of social interaction to effect a positive consequence on the levels of social and individual trust has a benign attraction, but it tells us little about how or why these norms, values and obligations associated with trust exist in the first place. Alternatively, the analysis of governmentality recognizes these discourses and social practices as the outcome of something more ordered. Not ordered in the sense of designed and managed but the consequence of what Foucault described as strategy: loosely connected sets of discourses and practices that follow a broad trajectory with no necessary correspondence between the different elements (Dreyfus and Rabinow 1982).

One tactic, increasingly used within the strategy of government as they struggle with the challenge of managing populations across an ever more complex range of social contexts, is the promotion of co-operative relations within different programmes and technologies. This works to promote, establish and maintain an ethic of co-operation and trustworthiness producing the trusting subject as a version of the disciplined subject, socially valued and malleable. Evidence of this can be found in a range of policy initiatives disseminated by national and local government drawing on communitarian discourses and including an endless array of devices promoting partnerships and active citizenship, e.g., Caring about Carers (DoH 1999), Choosing Health (DoH 2004), Independence, Well-being and Choice (DoH 2005). Devices targeting communities and neighbourhoods through initiatives promoting community activities often focused on a variety of locally based independent and autonomous groups. In areas where co-operative relations have failed and require rebuilding the deployment of discourses of empowerment is evident, inciting 'damaged subjects' to self-manage (Rose 1996). Located in initiatives such as Health Action Zones, Community Development Projects and Public Health activities a range of experts and lay volunteers work on individuals encouraging them to take responsibility for their health and engage in self-forming activities, self-care and self-help (Rose 1999).

Alongside this promotion of co-operative relationships, neo-liberal rule increasingly repositions the state as the coordinator of activity rather than the provider [cf. Modernising Social Services (DoH 1998), Every Child Matters (DoH 2003b), Choosing Health (DoH 2004) and Independence, Well-being and Choice (DoH 2005)], progressively drawing communities into the provision of welfare and the management of social problems (Clarke and Newman 1997, Rose 1996, 1999). New, often contradictory, rationalities of competition and co-operation, of participation and consumerism, substitute for earlier forms of public provision. Nevertheless, these contradictory rationalities maintain sufficient coherence to provide the basis for state intervention through professional and lay activity.

One such example is the restructured relationship between the private health sector and the British National Health Service [NHS] (DoH 2002, Lewis and Gillam 2003). Until recently, the private health sector distanced itself from the NHS arguing quality and choice while those committed to a public health service rejected private sector values. Now, a range of policy initiatives such as the use of private sector surgical facilities, the ability to have particular treatments at a facility chosen by the patient (DoH 2003a) and Private Finance Initiatives [PFIs] have blurred the boundaries between the public and private health sectors. Fixing large sections of the private sector as the reserve capacity of the NHS expanding and contracting on demand without the political consequences of public hospital closures. Furthermore, the use of private capital shifts fiscal liabilities from the present to the future while at the same time distancing the state from responsibility for the maintenance and refurbishment of hospital and other health service facilities and equipment.

Such developments suggest a re-articulation of the discursive structure of private, voluntary and statutory sector organisations in what Clarke and Newman (1997) describe as processes of colonisation and accommodation. Alongside State interventions aimed at provoking co-operative and trust-based relationships, such movements point to the way major institutions of society can become repositories of trust, providing both the example and the experience of trusting while also building the capacity for trust-based relationships across the social fabric. However, in contrast to functionalist conceptions of social institutions as repositories of trust, e.g., Misztal (1996), we need to identify the dynamic interplay between the state and the means of intervention at its disposal.

The challenges faced by the state over the last twenty-five years or so such as the increasing health costs of an aging population (Rose 1999, DoH 2005) have been matched by rapid social change. One effect of this has been the fragmentation of welfare away from a monolithic state organisation to one coordinated and financed by the state but disciplined by market mechanisms such as commissioning and competitive tendering (Clarke and Newman 1997, Lewis and Gillam 2003). Another effect has been the politicization of the technical, i.e., professional expertise (Johnson 2001), where a variety of forms of expertise competes for dominance. Under such conditions, trust is also politicized (Gilbert 1998). Trust becomes a commodity for exchange (Dasgupta 1988). Demanding new forms of governance and producing a paradox, autonomy for organisations and professionals released from direct management by the state is matched by ever more-complex forms of surveillance and control (Rose 1999, Gilbert 2001).

CONSTRUCTING PROFESSIONAL AUTHORITY THROUGH GOVERNMENTALITY

One feature of the established order in the last quarter of the last century was one where the institutionalized interests of state professionals were considered to stand in opposition to both the views of particular sections of the state and the newly produced subject position of 'welfare consumer' (Clarke and Newman 1997). Since the 1980s, claims of a decline in the authority of the professions accompanied this process. Public perceptions of failures of professional self-regulation articulate as institutionalized self-interest (Davies 2000), paralleled by the increasing power, or resistance, of health service users and welfare consumers to discipline professional activity. Managerialist techniques such as contracts and demands for transparency in exchanges unite managerial and user based discourses in an uncomfortable marriage (Rose 1999, Shaw 2001, Stewart and Wisniewski 2004, McIvor et al., 2002), frustrating the radical voice of user movements (Clarke and Newman 1997). Alongside, a massive increase in the access to the information, particularly through the internet, further complicates the situation. Specialist information, once the sole privilege of the professions, is now widely available, changing the relationship between professionals and laypersons once again challenging professional authority (Hardey 2005).

For Rose and Miller: 'governmentality is intrinsically linked to the activities of expertise, whose role is not weaving an all-pervasive web of "social control" but of enacting assorted attempts at the calculated administration of diverse aspects of conduct through countless, often competing, local tactics of education, persuasion, inducement, management, incitement, motivation and encouragement' (Rose and Miller 1992: 175). This web of activity and the specialized spaces created for expertise, work to construct professional authority, condensing the different levels of trust: interpersonal, systems and social capital; into the facework of experts. The fragmentation of expertise, once embedded in the directly managed institutions of the state, has enabled the dispersal of this expertise throughout the third sector leading to a re-articulation of the discourses that support professional activity and trust in expertise.

It is notable that despite the conflicts of the 1980s, the professions appear to carry on relatively unscathed leading to the conclusion that the decline in the authority, power and popularity of the professions has been overstated. One key factor is that certain tasks and activities demand professional competence especially in circumstances where the outcome cannot be pre-determined (Clarke and Newman 1997). Once again, revealing the paradox of autonomy and increasing regulation in the relationship between the state and professional activity. Returning to the earlier quotation from Foucault, what has occurred in this period is the re-articulation of government objectives and a re-structuring of the realms of professional jurisdiction and authority (Johnson 2001). Regulation and control of expertise through audits and contracts are disciplinary techniques that have modernized the tricky issue of governing professional activity. Accompanied by a re-articulation of professional discourse objectifying the activity of expertise rendering it both manageable (Rose 1999), and enabling the surveillance of professional activity across a landscape no longer defined by institutions and buildings of the poor law. At the same time policy documents such as 'Choosing Health' (DoH 2004) and Independence, Well-being and Choice (DoH 2005) are unashamedly consumerist, demonstrating shifts in the way community and population health is managed.

Central to this process is a paradox where the need for experts to manage complex and unpredictable situations has led to trust in professional autonomy becoming almost exclusively located with the management of risk (Rose 1996, 1999, Petersen 1997, Kemshall 2002). Competence in the management of risk is therefore the central basis, which maintains the professional status of health and social care professionals. Failure in this respect can lead to very public examinations of the competence of individual professionals, in particular where there is danger of a legitimation crisis. Professionals who, despite evidence of system failure, experience a form of symbolic sacrifice and public humiliation, recent examples include Dr Marietta Higgs [Cleveland Child Abuse Inquiry], Lisa Arthurworrey

[Victoria Climbie's social worker] (James 2005) and Professor Sir Roy Meadows [expert witness in child death cases (Laville 2005)].

Challenges to traditional or institutionalized expertise by new or non-conventional forms of expertise also demonstrates this re-structuring of the objectives of government and the jurisdiction of professionals. Some problems have persistently frustrated traditional forms of expertise in health care and social welfare at the same time widely dispersed and contract based activity enables entry for alternative approaches. Here again the dynamic quality of Governmentality, demonstrates processes of colonisation and accommodation. Lee-Treweek (2002) explores this process in the context of a complementary therapy, cranial osteopathy, describing how traditional medicine accepts elements of complementary practice on condition that the alternative approach accepts particular rituals and the primacy of the existing medical hierarchy. The need to manage chronic conditions such as skeletal and muscular pain, areas where traditional medicine has failed to provide a reliable treatment, enables a new form of expertise to institutionalise itself with the state. Securing trust in this specialized space enables this form of expertise to contest the hegemony of risk to its advantage.

What emerges is a fusion of consumerist, traditional, alternative and complementary discourses articulated with discourses of co-operation, partnership and trust in health and social care providing an matrix of spaces where a wider range of expertise, in both type and numerically, than ever before is embedded. At one level, experts identify risk at the same time as providing a general surveillance of the population, at another level they work within systems legitimated by a myriad of mechanisms of distrust while simultaneously working at another level on individuals to promote a general ethic of trust. Thus, the mechanisms constructing the contemporary authority of expertise are established. Condensing trust in the facework of experts places users of health and social care in a dynamic context. Health and social policy continually redefines previous patterns of social relationships both within health and welfare agencies and between those agencies and their customers. Gilbert et al. (2003) identified professionals in health and social care agencies responding to policy pressures by managing the expectations [trust] of different individuals and groups with potentially conflicting interest's, e.g., individual users, parents/carers and the local community. These experts engaged in a process of change and consolidation managing conflict while furthering both organisational and political aims related to community care. However, it is important to recognise, that the implementation of social policies are varied and policy implementation is highly contingent and uncertain (Lewis 2000, Watson 2000).

Conclusion

In the discussion of matrix inter-relationship trust, governmentality and professional expertise, I have acknowledged the contribution of a range of theorists to this increasingly important concept in the social sciences and in health and social care. We also note that the conceptualization of trust leads to confusion not only in the distinction between the bases of trust and the outcomes of trust, but also in the definition of what trust is and how trust can be differentiated from allied concepts such as confidence and familiarity. In addition, the recognition of the persistence of social and normatively based beliefs and values that act as synthetic, binding people into relationships that enable future orientated action is central to understanding the limitations of rational models of human behaviour and policy developed thereon. However, this theorising ignores identifying the mechanisms, which establish these trust-based values across the social fabric. These issues are of critical importance in health and social care. To address these pressures we explored Foucault's conceptual 'tool' of Governmentality thesis as the means to identify the role of trust in postmodernity, coupled with the processes for the employment of trust and the position of professional expertise in this process. A discursive framework promoting co-operative relations between individuals, communities and organisations consolidated this. This ethic is future orientated and promotes qualities and values that sustain trust-based relationships and forms of action. In the process of building co-operative relations, the role of professionals and professional authority is established.

Claims that trust in professionals has declined is not substantiated given the pivotal role professionals continue to play in health and social care rather the reconfiguration of political objectives has changed the relationship between professionals and the state. The fact that some professional groups have found the process traumatic merely reinforces our claim that trust is politized, contested and functions as a commodity.

The challenge for research and practice in health and social care is to move away from viewing trust as a benign side effect of human activity. Instead, we should be clear that trust is the intended outcome of a range of social policies and the discourses and practices that underpin those policies whose aim is the management of a population that is useful, productive and self-managing. Therefore, we need to focus on the interplay between social policy and the lives of individuals, families or groups and communities. Drawing out the costs and benefits of trust-based relationships, identifying the way the facework of experts maintains the legitimacy of systems while simultaneously promoting social cohesion, and constructing professional authority. We require an analysis the micro-politics of trust, played out in a myriad of interactions between users, carers, volunteers, professionals and administrators, within health and social care. In addition, we have to identify the discourses and practices, e.g., the distinction between trust and hope, that underpin this activity and the consequences of trust-based relationships for those involved. However, what has not been delineated sufficiently has been the relationship between narrative approaches to the life course.

There has been an increasing interest in aging and family, within sociological developments relating to aging and social policy since the late 1990s (Minkler, 1998). This is a trend that has cut across Canadian, American and European research (Cloke et al., 2006; Walker and Naegele, 1999; Minkler, 1998; Bengtson et al., 2000; Biggs and Powell, 2001; Carmel et al., 2007). The reasons for such expansion are as much economic and political as they are academic. US and European governments recognize that the "family" is important for social and economic needs and this should be reflected in our understanding of aging, family processes and in social policy (Beck, 2005). This leads to the question: how can we theoretically contextualize this and what are lessons for family research in sociological theorizing?

"Narrativity" has become established in the social sciences, both as a method of undertaking and interpreting research (cf Kenyon et al., 1999; Holstein and Gubrium, 2000; Biggs et al., 2003) and as a technique for modifying the self (McAdams, 1993; Mcleod, 1997). Both Gubrium (1992) and Katz (1999) suggest that older people construct their own analytical models of personal identity based on lived experience and on narratives already existing in their everyday environments. By using a narrative approach, the meaning of family can be told through stories about the self as well as ones "at large" in public discourse.

"Discourse" is a phrase more often used to denote a relatively fixed set of stories that individuals or groups have to conform to in order to take up a recognized and legitimate role. Such an understanding of discourse can be found in the earlier work of Michel Foucault (1977) and others (Powell and Biggs, 2001). Self-storying, draws attention to the ways in which family identities are both more open to negotiation and are more likely to be "taken in" in the sense of being owned and worked on by individuals themselves. Families, of course, are made up of interpersonal relationships within and between generations that are subject to both the formal rhetoric of public discourse, and the self-stories that bind them together in everyday life. The notion of family is, then, an amalgam of policy discourse and everyday negotiation and as such alerts us to the wider social implications of those relationships (cf Powell, 2005).

The rhetoric of social policy and the formal representations of adult aging and family life that one finds there, provide a source of raw material for the construction of identity and a series of spaces in which such identities can be legitimately performed. It is perhaps not overstating the case to say that the "success" of a family policy can be judged from the degree to which people live within the stories or narratives of family created by it.

In fact, the relationship between families and older people has been consecutively re-written in the social policy literature. Each time a different story has been told and different aspects of the relationship have been thrown into high relief. It might even be argued that the family has become a key site upon which expected norms of intergenerational relations and late-life citizenship are being built. This paper explores the significance of such narratives, using developments in the UK as a case example that may also shed light on wider contemporary issues associated with old age.

The structure of the paper is fourfold. Firstly, we start by mapping out the emergence and consolidation of neoliberal family policy and its relationship to emphasis on family obligation, state surveillance and active citizenship. Secondly, we highlight both the ideological continuities and discontinuities of the subsequent social democratic turn and their effects on older people and the family. Thirdly, research studies are drawn on to highlight how "grand-parenting" has been recognized by governments in recent years, as a particular way of "storying" the relationship between old age and family life. Finally, we explore ramifications for researching family policy and old age by pointing out that narratives of inclusion and exclusion often co-exist. It is suggested that in future, aging and family life will include the need to negotiate multiple policy narratives. At an interpersonal level, sophisticated narrative strategies would be required if a sense of familial continuity and solidarity is to be maintained.

NEOLIBERALISM, AGING, AND THE FAMILY

Political and social debate since the Reagan/Thatcher years, has been dominated by neoliberalism, which postulates the existence of autonomous, assertive, rational individuals who must be protected and liberated from "big government" and state interference (Gray, 1995). Indeed, Walker and Naegele (1999) claim a startling continuity across Europe is the way "the family" has been positioned by governments as these ideas have spread beyond their original "English speaking" base.

Neoliberal policies on the family, has almost always started from a position of *laissez-faire*, excepting when extreme behavior threatens its members or wider social relations (Beck, 2005). Using the UK as a case example, it can be seen that that neoliberal policy came to focus on two main issues. And, whilst both only represent the point at which a minimalist approach from the state touches family life, they come to mark the dominant narrative through which aging and family are made visible in the public domain (Cloke et al., 2006).

On the one hand, increasing attention was paid to the role families took in the care of older people who were either mentally or physically infirm. A series of policy initiatives (UKG, 1981, 1989, 1990) recognized that families were a principal source of care and support. "Informal" family care became a key building block of policy toward an aging population. It both increased the salience of traditional family values, independence from government and enabled a reduction in direct support from the state.

On the other hand, helping professionals, following US experience (Pillemer and Wolf, 1986), became increasingly aware of the abuse that older people might suffer and the need to protect vulnerable adults from a variety of forms of abuse and neglect (Biggs et al., 1995). Policy guidance, *"No Longer Afraid: the safe-guard of older people in domestic settings,"* was issued in 1993, shortly after the move to seeing informal care as the mainstay of the welfare of older people. As the title suggests, this was also directed primarily at the family.

It is perhaps a paradox that a policy based ostensibly on the premises of leaving-be, combines two narrative streams that result in increased surveillance of the family. This paradox is based largely on these points being the only ones where policy "saw" aging in families, rather than ignoring it. This is not to say that real issues of abuse and neglect fail to exist, even though UK politicians have often responded to them as if they were some form of natural disaster unrelated to the wider policy environment. To understand the linking of these narratives, it is important to examine trends tacit in the debate on family and aging, but central to wider public policy.

Wider economic priorities, to "roll back the state" and thereby release re-sources for individualism and free enterprise, had become translated into a family discourse about caring obligations and the need to enforce them. If families ceased to care, then the state would have to pick up the bill. It was not that families were spoken of as being naturally abusive. Neither was the "discovery" of familial abuse linked to community care policy outside academic debate (Biggs, 1996). Discourses on the rise of abuse and on informal care remained separate in the formal policy domain. However, a subtle change of narrative tone had taken place. Families, rather than being seen as "havens against a harsh world," were now easily perceived as potential sites of mistreatment, and the previously idealized role of the unpaid carer became that of a potential recalcitrant, attempting to avoid their family obligations. An attempt to protect a minority of abused elders thus took the shape of a tacit threat, hanging above the head of every aging family (Biggs and Powell, 2000). It is worth note that these policy developments took little account of research evidence indicating that family solidarity and a willingness to care had decreased in neither the UK (Wenger, 1994; Phillipson, 1998) nor the US (Bengtson and Achenbaum, 1993). Further, it appeared that familial caring was actually moving away from relationships based on obligation and toward ones based on negotiation (Finch and Mason, 1993).

Family commitment has, for example, to vary depending upon the characteristic care-giving patterns within particular families. Individualistic families provided less instrumental help and made use of welfare services, whereas a second, collectivist pattern offered greater personal support. Whilst this study focused primarily on upward generational support, Silverstein and Bengtson (1997) observed that "tight-knit" and "detached" family styles were often common across generations. Unfortunately, policy developments have rarely taken differences in care-giving styles into account, preferring a general narrative of often idealized role relation-ships. It is not unfair to say that during the neoliberal period, the dominant narrative of family became that of a site of care going wrong.

SOCIAL DEMOCRACY, AGING, AND THE FAMILY

Social democratic policies toward the family arose from the premise that by the early 1990s, the free-market policies of the Thatcher/Reagan years had seriously damaged the social fabric of the nation state and that its citizens needed to be encouraged to identify again with the national project.

A turn to an alternative, sometimes called "the third way," emerging under Clinton, Blair and Schroeder administrations in the US and parts of Europe, attempted to find means of mending that social fabric, and as part of it, relations between older people and their families (Beck, 2005). The direction that the new policy narrative took is summarized in UK Prime Minister Blair's (1996) statement that "the most meaningful stake anyone can have in society is the ability to earn a living and support a family." Work, or failing that, work-like activities, plus an active contribution to family life began slowly to emerge, delineating new narratives within which to grow old (Hardill et al., 2007).

Giddens (1998) in the UK and Beck (1998) in Germany, both proponents of social democratic politics, have claimed that citizens are faced with the task of piloting themselves and their families through a changing world in which globalization has transformed our relations with each other, now based on avoiding risk. According to Giddens (1998), a new partnership is needed between government and civil society. Government support to the renewal of community through local initiative, would gives an increasing role to "voluntary" organizations, encourages social entrepreneurship and significantly, supports the "democratic" family characterized by "equality, mutual respect, autonomy, decision-making through communication and freedom of violence." It is argued that social policy should be less concerned with "equality" and more with "inclusion," with community participation reducing the moral and financial hazard of dependence (cf Walker, 2002; Biggs et al., 2003; Powell and Owen, 2007; Walker and Aspalter, 2008).

Through an increased awareness of the notion of ageism, the influence of European ideas about social inclusion and North American social communitarianism, families and older people found themselves transformed into active citizens who should be encouraged to participate in society, rather than be seen as a potential burden upon it (Biggs, 2001). A contemporary UK policy document, entitled *"Building a Better Britain for Older People"* (DSS, 1998) is typical of a new genre of western policy, re-storying the role of older adults:

"The contribution of older people is vital, both to families, and to voluntary organisations and charities. We believe their roles as mentors—providing ongoing support and advice to families, young people and other older people—should be recognised. Older people already show a considerable commitment to volunteering. The Government is working with voluntary groups and those representing older people to see how we can increase the quality and quantity of opportunities for older people who want to volunteer."

What is perhaps striking about this piece is that it is one of the few places where families are mentioned in an overview on older people, with the exception of a single mention of carers, many of whom, it is pointed out, "are pensioners themselves." In both cases the identified role for older people constitutes a reversal of the narrative offered in preceding policy initiatives. The older person like other members of family structure is portrayed as an active member of the *social milieu*, offering care and support to others (Hardill et al., 2007).

The dominant preoccupation of this policy initiative, is not however, concerned with families. Rather, there is a change of emphasis toward the notion of aging as an issue of lifestyle, and as such draws on contemporary gerontological observations of the "blurring" of age-based identities (Featherstone and Hepworth, 1995) and the growth of the grey consumer (Katz, 1999).

Whilst such a narrative is attractive to pressure groups, voluntary agencies and, indeed, social gerontologists; there is, just as with the policies of the neoliberals, an underlying economic motive which may or may not be to the long term advantage to older people and their families. Again, as policies develop, the force driving the story of elders as active citizens was to be found in policies of a fiscal nature. The most likely place to discover how the new story of aging, fits the bigger picture is in government-wide policy. In this case the document has been entitled *"Winning the Generation Game"* (UKG, 2000a). This begins well with "One of the most important tasks for twenty-first century Britain is to unlock the talents and potential of all its citizens. Everyone has a valuable contribution to make, throughout their lives." However, the reasoning behind this statement becomes clearer when policy is explained in terms of a changing demographic profile: "With present employment rates" it is argued, "one million more over-50s would not be working by 2020 because of growth in the older population. There will be 2 million fewer working-age people under 50 and 2 million more over 50: a shift equivalent to nearly 10 percent of the total working population."

The solution, then, is to engage older people not only part of family life but also in work, volunteering or mentoring. Older workers become a reserve labor pool, filling the spaces left by falling numbers of younger workers. They thus contribute to the economy as producers as well as consumers and make fewer demands on pensions and other forms of support. Those older people who are not thereby socially included, can engage in the work-like activity of volunteering.

Most of these policy narratives only indirectly affect the aging family. Families only have a peripheral part to play in the story, and do not appear to be central to the lives of older people. However, it is possible to detect the same logic at work when attention shifts from the public to the private sphere. Here the narrative stream develops the notion of "grand-parenting" as a means of social inclusion. This trend can be found in the UK, in France (Girard and Ogg, 1998), Germany (Scharf and Wenger, 1995), as well as in the USA (Minkler, 1999).

In the UK context the most detailed reference to grand-parenting can be found in an otherwise rather peculiar place—namely from the Home Office—an arm of British Government primarily concerned with law and order. In a document entitled *"Supporting Families"* (2000b), "family life" we are told, "is the foundation on which our communities, our society and our country are built." "Business people, people from the community, students and grandparents" are encouraged to join a schools mentoring network. Further, "the interests of grandparents, and the contribution they make, can be marginalized by service providers who, quite naturally, concentrate on dealing with parents. We want to change all this and encourage grandparents—and other relatives—to play a positive role in their families." By which it is meant: "home, school links or as a source of social and cultural history" and support when "nuclear families are under stress." Even older people who are not themselves grandparents can join projects "in which volunteers act as "grandparents" to contribute their experience to a local family."

In the narratives of social democracy, the aging family is seen as a reservoir of potential social inclusion. Older people are portrayed as holding a key role in the stability of both the public sphere, through work and volunteering, and in the private sphere, primarily through grandparental support and advice (Cloke et al., 2006). Grandparents, in particular, are storied as mentors and counselors across the public and private spheres.

Whilst the grandparental title has been used as a catch-all within the dominant policy narrative; bringing with it associations of security, stability and an in many ways an easier form of relationship than direct parenting; it exists as much in public as in private space. It is impossible to interpret this construction of grandparenthood without placing it in the broader project of social inclusion, itself a response to increased social fragmentation and economic competition. Indeed it may not be an exaggeration to refer this construal of grand-parenting as neofamilial. In other words, the grandparent has out-grown the family as part of a policy search to include older adults in wider society. The grandparent becomes a mentor to both parental and grandparental generations as advice is not restricted to schools and support in times of stress, but also through participation in the planning of amenities and public services (BGOP, 2000).

This is a very different narrative of older people and their relationship to families, from that of the dependent and burdensome elder. In the land of policy conjuring, previously conceived problems of growing economic expense and social uselessness have been miraculously reversed. Older people are now positioned as the solution to problems of demographic change, rather than their cause. They are a source of guidance to ailing families, rather than their victims. Both narratives increase the social inclusion of a potentially marginal social group: formerly known as the elderly.

"GRAND-PARENTING" POLICY

There is much to be welcomed in this story of the active citizen elder. Especially so if policy-inspired discourse and lived self-narratives are taken to be one and the same. There are also certain problems, however, if the two are unzipped, particularly when the former is viewed through the lens of what we know about families from other sources.

First, each of the roles identified in the policy domain, volunteering, mentor-ship and grand-parenting, have a rather second–hand quality. By this is meant that each is supportive to another player who is central to the task at hand. Rather like within Erikson's psycho-social model of the lifecycle, the role allocated to older people approximates grand-generativity and thereby contingent upon the earlier, but core life task of generativity itself (Kivnick, 1988). In other words it is contingent upon an earlier part of life and the narratives woven around it, and fails to distinguish an authentic element of the experience of aging.

When the roles are examined in this light, a tacit secondary status begins to emerge. Volunteering becomes unpaid work; mentoring, support to helping professionals in their eroded pastoral capacities; and grand-parenting, in its familial guise, a sort of peripheral parent without the hassle. This peripherality may be in many ways desirable, so long as there is an alternative pole of authentic attraction that ties the older adult into the *social milieux*. Either that or the narrative should allow space for legitimized withdrawal from socially inclusive activities. Unfortunately the dominant policy narrative has little to say on either count.

Second, there is a shift of attention away from the most frail and oldest old, to a third age of active or positive aging, which, incidentally, may or may not take place in families. It is striking that a majority of policy documents of what might be called the "new aging," start counting from age 50, an observation that is true for formal government rhetoric and pressure from agencies and initiatives lead by elders (Biggs, 2001). This interpretation of the life-course has been justified in terms of its potential for forming intergenerational alliances (BGOP, 2000) and fits well with the economic priority of drawing on older people as a reserve labor force (UKG, 2000b).

Third, there is a striking absence of analysis of family relations at that age. Possibilities of intergenerational conflict as described in other literature (De Beauvoir, 1979), not least in research into three-generation family therapy (Hargrave and Anderson, 1992; Qualls, 1999), plus the everyday need for tact in negotiating childcare roles (Bornat et al., 1999; Waldrop et al., 1999), appear not to have been taken into account. This period in the aging life-course is often marked by midlife tension and multi-generational transitions, such as those experienced by late adolescent children and by an increasingly frail top generation (Ryff and Seltzer, 1996). Research has indicated that solidarity between family generations is not uniform, and will involve a variety of types and degrees of intimacy and reciprocity (Silverstein and Bengtson, 1997).

Finally, little consideration has been given to the potential conflict between the tacit hedonism of aging lifestyles based on consumption and those more socially inclusive roles of productive contribution, of which the "new grand-parenting" has become an important part. Whilst there are few figures on grandparental activity it does, for example, appear that community volunteering amongst older people is embraced with much less enthusiasm than policy-makers would wish (Boaz et al., 1999). Chambre (1993) claims volunteering in the US diminishes in old age. Her findings indicate the highest rates of volunteering occur in mid-life, where nearly two thirds volunteer. This rate declines to 47 percent for persons aged between 65 and 74 and to 32 percent among persons 75 and over. A UK Guardian-ICM (2000) poll of older adults indicated that, amongst grandfathers, but not grandmothers, there was a degree of suspicion of child-care to support their own children's family arrangements. More than a quarter of men expressed this concern, compared with only 19 percent of women interviewed. The UK charity, Age Concern, stated: "One in ten grandparents are under the age of 56. They have 10 more years of work and are still leading full lives."

One might speculate, immersed in this narrative stream, that problematic family roles and relationships cease to exist for the work-returning, volunteering and community enhancing 50-plus "elder." Indeed, the major protagonists of social democracy seem blissfully unaware of several decades of research, particularly feminist research, demonstrating the mythical status of the "happy family" (cf, e.g., Land, 1999).

What emerges from research literature on grand-parenting as it is included in people's everyday experience and narratives of self, indicates two trends: (1) there appears to be a general acceptance of the positive value of relatively loose and undemanding exchange between first and third generations, and (2) that deep commitments become active largely in situations of extreme family stress or breakdown of the middle generation.

First, grandparents have potential to influence and develop children through the transmission of values. Subsequently, grand-parents serve as arbiters of knowledge and transmit knowledge that is unique to their identity, life experience and history. In addition, grandparents can become mentors, performing the function of a generic life guide for younger children. This "transmission" role is confirmed by Mills' (1999) study of mixed gender relations and by Waldrop et al.'s (1999) report on grandfathering. According to Roberto (1990) early research on grand-parenting in the USA has attempted to identify the roles played by grandparents within the family system and towards grandchildren. Indeed, much US work on grand-parenting has focused on how older adults view and structure their relationships with younger people.

African American grandparents, for example, take a more active role, correcting the behavior of grandchildren and acting like "protectors" of the family. Accordingly, such behaviors are related to effects of divorce and under/unemployment. Research by Kennedy (1990) indicates, however, that there is a cultural void when it comes to grand-parenting roles for many white families with few guide-lines on how they should act as grandparents.

Girard and Ogg (1998) report that grand-parenting is a rising political issue in French family policy. They note that most grandmothers welcome the new role they have in child care of their grandchildren, but there is a threshold beyond which support interferes with their other commitments. Contact between older parents and their grandchildren is less frequent that with youngsters, with financial support becoming more prominent.

Two reports, explicitly commissioned to inform UK policy (Hayden et al., 1999; Boaz et al., 1999) classify grand-parenting under the general rubric of intergenerational relationships. Research evidence is cited, that "when thinking about the future, older people looked forward to their role as grandparents" and that grandparents looked after their grandchildren and provided them with "love, support and a listening ear," providing childcare support to their busy children and were enthusiastic about these roles.

Hayden et al. (1999) used focus groups and qualitative interviewing and report that: "grand-parenting included spending time with grandchildren both in active and sedentary hobbies and pursuits, with many participants commenting on the mental and physical stimulation they gained from sharing activities with the younger generation. Coupled with this, the Beth Johnson Foundation (1998) found that older people as mentors had increased levels of participation with more friends and engendered more social activity. With the exception of the last study, each has relied on exclusive self-report data, or views on what grand-parenting might be like at some future point.

In research from the tradition of examining social networks, and thus not overtly concerned with the centrality of grand-parenting or grandparent-like roles as such, it is rarely identified as a key relationship and could not be called a strong theme. Studies on the UK, (Phillipson et al., 2000), Japan (Izuhara, 2000), the US (Schreck, 2000; Minkler, 1999), Hispanic Americans (Freidenberg, 2000), and Germany, (Chamberlayne and King, 2000) provide little evidence that grand-children, as distinct from adult children, are prominent members of older peoples reported social networks.

Grandparental responsibility becomes more visible if the middle generation is for some reason absent. Thompson, (1999) reports from the UK, that when parents part or die, it is often grandparents who take up supporting, caring and mediating roles on behalf of their grandchildren. The degree of involvement was contingent however on the quality of emotional closeness and communication within the family group. Minkler, (1999) has indicated that in the US, one in ten grandparents has primary responsibility for raising a grandchild at some point, with care often lasting for several years.

This trend varies between ethnic groups, with 4.1 percent White, 6.55 percent Hispanic and 13.55 African American children living with their grandparents or other relatives. It is argued that a 44 percent increase in such responsibilities is connected to the devastating effects of wider social issues, including AIDS/HIV, drug abuse, parental homelessness and prison policy. Thomson and Minkler (2001) note that there is an increasing divergency in the meaning of grand-parenting between different socio-economic groups, with extensive care-givers (7 percent of the sampled population) having increasingly fewer characteristics in common with the 14.9 percent who did not provide child-care. In the UK, a similar split has been identified with 1 percent of British grandparents becoming extensive caregivers, against a background pattern of occasional or minimal direct care (Duckworth, 2001).

It would appear that grand-parenting is not, then a uniform phenomenon, and extensive grand-parenting or grandparent-like activities are rarely an integral part of social inclusion. Rather, whilst it is seen as providing some intergenerational benefit, it may be a phenomenon that requires an element of un-intrusiveness and negotiation in its non-extensive form. When extensively relied on it is more likely to be a response to severely eroded inclusive environments and the self-protective reactions of families living with them. Minkler's analysis draws attention to race as a feature of social exclusion that is poorly handled by policy narratives afforded to the family and old age. There is a failure to recognize structural forms of inequality, and action seeking to socially include older people as a category appears to draw heavily on the occasional helper and social volunteer as a dominant narrative.

Towards Diverse Narrative Streams?

Each phase of social policy, be it the Reagan/Thatcherite neoliberalism of the 1980s and early 1990s, the Clinton/Blairite interpretation of social democracy in the late 90s, or the millennial Bush administration, leaves a legacy. Moreover, policy development is uneven and subject to local emphasis and elision, which means that it is quite possible for different, even conflicting narratives of family and later life to coexist in different parts of the policy system. Each period generates a discourse that can legitimate the lives of older people and family relations in particular ways, and as their influence accrues, create the potential of entering into multiple narrative streams.

A striking feature of recent policy history has been that not only have the formal policies been quite different in their tenor and tacit objectives, one from another, they have also addressed different areas of the lives of aging families. Where there is little narrative overlap there is the possibility of both policies existing, however opposed they may be ideologically or in terms of practical outcome. Different narratives may colonize different parts of policy, drawing on bureaucratic inertia, political inattention and convenience to maintain their influence. They have a living presence, not least when they impinge on personal aging.

Also, both policy discourses share a deep coherence, which may help to explain their co-existence. Each offers a partial view of aging and family life whilst downloading risk and responsibility onto aging families and aging identities. Neither recognizes aging which is not secondary to an independent policy objective. Both mask the possibility of authentic tasks of aging.

If the analysis outlined above is accepted, then it is possible to see contemporary social policy addressing diverse aspects of the family life of older people in differing and contradictory ways. Contradictory narratives for the aging family exist in a landscape that is a one and the same time increasingly blurred in terms of roles and relationships and split-off in terms of narrative coherence and consequences for identity. Indeed in a future of complex and multiple policy agendas, it would appear that a narrative of social inclusion through active aging can coexist with one emphasizing carer obligation and surveillance. Such a co-existence may occasionally become inconvenient at the level of public rhetoric. However, at an experiential and ontological level, that is to say at the level of the daily lives of older adults and their families, the implications may become particularly acute. Multiple co-existing policy narratives may become a significant source of risk to identity maintenance within the aging family.

One has to imagine a situation in which later lives are lived, skating on a surface of legitimizing discourse. For everyday intents and purposes this surface supplies the ground on which one can build an aging identity, relate to other family members and immediate community. However, there is always the possibility of slipping, of being subject to trauma or transition. Serious slippage will provoke being thrown onto a terrain that had previously been hidden, an alternative narrative of aging with entirely different premises, relationship expectations and possibilities for personal expression.

Policy narratives, however, are also continually breaking down and fail to achieve hegemony as they encounter lived experience. Indeed, it could be argued that a continuous process of re-constitution takes place via the play of competing narratives. When we are addressing the issue of older people's identity in later life we can usefully note Foucault's (1977) contention that there has been a growth in attempts to control national populations through discourses of normality, but at the same time this has entailed increasing possibilities for self-government.

Part of the attractiveness of thinking in terms of narrative, that policies tell us stories that we don't have necessarily to believe, is the opening of a critical distance between description and intention. Policy narratives describe certain, often idealized, states of affairs. Depicting them as stories, rather than realities, allows the interrogation of the space between that description and experience (cf Powell, 2005).

CONCLUSION

What does this examination of social policy discourse and everyday stories of aging tell us, and what are the lessons for future sociological research?

Firstly, we are alerted to the partial nature of the narratives supplied by social policy, which affects our perception of families as well as of older people. The simplifying role of policy discourse tends to highlight certain, politically valued, aspects of experience to the exclusion of other possibilities. These are also the discourses most likely to be reflected in policy-sponsored research.

Secondly, the inclusion of certain roles, activities and age bands in policy discourse has a legitimizing role. In other words, it not only sanctions the direction of resources and the action of helping professionals important though that is. It also contributes to the legitimated identities afforded to people in later life. This includes at least two factors key to aging identity: the creation of social spaces in which to perform aging roles and be recognized as such, and, the supply of material with which explicit yet personal narratives of self and family can be made.

Thirdly, a significant element in the "riskiness" of building aging and family identities under contemporary conditions may arise from the existence of multiple policy discourses that personal narratives, of family, self and relations between the two, have to negotiate. Research on the management of identity, should, then, be sensitized to the multiple grounds on which identity might be built and the potential sources of conflict and uncertainty may bring.

Fourthly, attention should be paid to the relationship between tacit and explicit influences on identity management in late-life families. The multiple sources for building stories "to live by" and the tension between legitimizing discourses and alternative narratives of self and family, would suggest that identities are managed at different levels, for different audiences and at different levels of awareness.

REFERENCES

Baltes, M. and Carstensen, L. (1996). 'The process of successful ageing', *Ageing and Society*, 16: 397-422.

Beck, L. (2005). 'Still-growing China faces crisis supporting ageing population', *The Scotsman*, 5th January.

Beck, U. (1992). *Risk Society: Towards a New Modernity.* London: Sage.

Beck, U. (1998). *Democracy Without Enemies*, Polity: Cambridge, UK.

Beck, U. (2005). *Power and Countervailing Power in the Global Age.* Cambridge: Polity.

Bell, V. (2002). The Vigilant[e] Parent and the Paedophile: The News of the World campaign 2000 and the contemporary governmentality of child sexual abuse. *Feminist Theory*, 3(1): 83 – 102.

Bengtson, V.L. and Achenbaum, W. (1993). *The Changing Contract Across Generations*, Aldine De Gruyter: New York.

Bengtson, V.L. and Lowenstein, A. (Eds.) (2004). *Global Aging and Challenges to Families*. New York: De Gruyter.

Bengtson, V.L., Giarrusso, R., Silverstein, M. and Wang, H. (2000). Families and Intergenerational Relationships in Aging Societies, *Hallym International Journal of Aging*, Vol. 2, No. 1, pp. 3-10.

BGOP, Better Government of Older People (2000). *Better Government for Older People*, BGOP: Wolverhampton, UK.

Biggs, S. (1993). *Understanding ageing*, Milton Keynes: Open University Press.

Biggs, S. (1996). A Family Concern: Elder Abuse in British Social Policy, *Critical Social Policy*, Vol. 16, No. 2, pp. 63-88.

Biggs, S. (2001). Toward Critical Narrativity: Stories of Aging in Contemporary Social Policy, *Journal of Aging Studies*, Vol. 15, pp. 1-14.

Biggs, S. and Powell, J. (2000). Surveillance and Elder Abuse: The Rationalities and Technologies of Community Care, *Journal of Contemporary Health*, Vol. 4, No. 1, pp. 43-49.

Biggs, S. and Powell, J.L. (2001). 'A Foucauldian analysis of old age and the power of social welfare', *J Aging Soc Policy*; 12, 2:93-112.

Biggs, S., Estes, C., and Phillipson, C. (2003). *Social Theory, Social Policy and Ageing*, Open University Press: Buckingham, UK.

Biggs, S., Phillipson, C., and Kingston, P. (1995). *Elder Abuse in Perspective*, Open University Press: Buckingham, UK.

BJF, Beth Johnson Foundation. (1999). *Intergenerational Programmes*, BJF: Stoke, UK.

Blair, T. (1996). *New Britain: My Vision of a Young Country*, Fourth Estate: Lon-don.

Boaz, A., Hayden, C., and Bernard, M. (1999). Attitudes and Aspirations of Older People. *DSS Research Report*, No. 101, CDS: London.

Bornat, J., Dimmock, B., Jones, D., and Peace, S. (1999). Stepfamilies and Older People, *Ageing and Society*, Vol. 19, No. 2, pp. 239-62.

Brownlie, J., & Howson, A. (2005). 'Leaps of Faith' and MMR: An Empirical study of trust, *Sociology*, 39(2): 221 – 239.

Building blocks (2004). *Africa-wide briefing notes – supporting older carers*, HIV AIDS Alliance and Help Age International.

Burchell, G. (1991). *The Foucault Effect: Studies in Governmentality*. London: Harvester Wheatsheaf.

Butler, J. (1993). *Bodies that matter: on the discursive limits of 'sex'*, London: Routledge.

Butler, J. (1998). *The psychic life of power: theories in subjection*, Stanford, CA: Stanford University Press.

References

Bytheway, B. (1995). *Ageism*, Milton Keynes: Open University Press.

Carmel, S., Morse, C.A., and Torres-Gil, F.M. (eds.) (2007). *Lessons on Aging from Three Nations*, Baywood: New York.

Chamberlayne, P. and King, A. (2000). *Cultures of Care*, Policy Press: London.

Chambre, S.M. (1993). Volunteerism by Elders: Past Traditions and Future Prospects, *The Gerontologist*, Vol. 33, pp. 221-28.

Chen, Shasha. (2006). 'Beijing has fewer children and more seniors', *Beijing Today*, 24th March.

China Daily. (2004). 'Tailoring health care policies for the elderly', April 5th.

China Statistical Yearbook 2005, Beijing: China Statistics Press.

Clarke, J. & Newman, J. (1997). *The Managerial State*. London: Sage.

Cloke, P., Johnsen, S., and May, J. (2006). Ethical citizenship? Volunteers and the ethics of providing services for homeless people *Geoforum* 38(6): 1089-1101.

Cook, I.G. and Dummer, T.J.B. (2004). 'Changing health in China: re-evaluating the epidemiological transition model', *Health Policy*, 67, 3: 329-43.

Cook, I.G. and Powell, J.L. (2003). 'Active aging and China: a critical excursion', *Syncronia*, Summer.

Cook, I.G. and Powell, J.L. (2005a). 'China, aging and social policy: the influences and limitations of the bio-medical paradigm', *Journal of Societal and Social Policy*, 4, 2: 71-89.

Cook, I.G. and Powell, J.L. (2005b). *China and Ageing: the influences of the bio-medical paradigm on population discourse and health policy*, Paper to the China Session, 'Continuity, transition and transcendence: urban development and reform in China (2),', RGS/IBG Annual Conference, September.

Cook, I.G. and Powell, J.L. (2007) *New Perspectives on China and Aging*. Nova Science Publishers, Inc.: New York.

Dasgupta, P. (1988). Trust as a commodity, in Gambetta, D. (ed.) *Making and Breaking Co-operative Relations*. Oxford: Basil Blackwell.

Davidson, A. (1994). Ethics as ascetics: Foucault, the history of ethics, and ancient thought. In C, Gutting [ed.] *The Cambridge Companion to Foucault.* Cambridge: Cambridge University Press.

Davies, C. (2000). The Demise of Professional Self-regulation: A moment to mourn? In Lewis, G., Gewirtz, S and Clarke, J., [eds.] *Rethinking Social Policy.* London: Sage pp 276 – 289.

Davies, H. (1999). Falling Public Trust in Health Services: implications for accountability. *Journal of Health Services Research and Policy*: 4(4): 193 - 194.

De Beauvoir, S. (1979). *Old Age*, Penguin: London.

Dean, H. (2003). The Third Way and Social Welfare: The Myth of Post-emotionalism. *Social Policy and Administration,* 37(7): 679 - 708.

Department of Health. (1998). *Modernising Social Services Cm 4169.* London: The Stationery Office.

Department of Health. (1999). *Caring about Carers: A national strategy for carers.* London: Department of Health.

Department of Health. (2002). *Growing Capacity: A New Role for External Health Care Providers in England.* Department of Health: London.

Department of Health. (2003a). *Building on the best: Choice, Responsiveness and Equality in the NHS Cm 6079.* London: The Stationery office.

Department of Health. (2003b). *Every Child Matters Cm 5860.* London: The Stationery Office.

Department of Health. (2004). *Choosing Health: Making Health Choices Easier Cm 6374.* London: The Stationery Office.

Department of Health. (2005). *Independence, Well-being and Choice Cm 6499.* London: The Stationery Office.

Dreyfus H. L. & Rabinow, P. (1982). *Michel Foucault: Beyond Structuralism and Hermeneutics.* London: Harvester Wheatsheaf.

DSS, Department of Social Security (1998). *Building a Better Britain for Older People*, HMSO: London.

Du, P. and Tu, P. (2000). 'Population Ageing and Old Age Security', chapter in in Peng X. and Guo Z. (eds), *The Changing Population of China*, Oxford: Blackwell, pp. 77-90.

References

Duckworth, L. (2001). Grandparents Who Bring Up Children Need More Help, *Independent*, September 13.

Durkheim, E. (1964). *The Rules of Sociological Method*. New York: Free Press.

Epstein, H. (2001). 'Time of Indifference', *New York Review of Books,* April 12, pp. 33- 38.

Estes, C. (2001). *Social Policy and Aging*. Sage: Thousand Oaks.

Estes, C., Biggs, S. and Phillipson, C. (2003). *Social Theory, Social Policy and Ageing*. Open University Press: Milton Keynes.

Featherstone, M. and Hepworth, M. (1993). Images of Positive Ageing, in M. Featherstone and A. Wernick (eds.), *Images of Ageing*, Routledge: London.

Federal Reserve Bank of Kansas City (2004). *Global Demographic Change: Economic Impacts and Policy Challenges. Symposium proceedings*. August 26–28, 2004. Available at: http://www.kc.frb.org/Publicat/sympos/2004/sym04prg.htm.

Finch, J. and Mason, J. (1993). *Negotiating Family Responsibilities*, Routledge: London.

Foucault, M. (1972). *The archaeology of knowledge*, London: Tavistock.

Foucault, M. (1977). *Discipline and Punish*, Tavistock: London.

Foucault, M. (1979). 'On governmentality', *Ideology and Consciousness* 6: 5-12.

Freidenberg, J. (2000). *Growing Old in EL Barrio*, New York University Press: New York.

Fukuyama F. (1996). *Trust: the social virtues and the creation of prosperity*. Harmondsworth: Penguin.

Gavrilov, L. and Gavrilova, N. (1991). *The Biology of Life Span: A Quantitative Approach*. New York: Harwood Academic Publisher.

Giddens A. (1990). *Consequences of Modernity*. Stanford NY: Stanford University Press.

Giddens A. (1991). *Modernity and Self-Identity: Self and Society in the Late Modern Age*. Bristol: Polity Press.

Giddens, A. (1993) *Sociology*. Cambridge Polity Press.

Giddens, A. (1994). Living in a post-traditional society, in U Beck, A Giddens & S Lash [eds.] *Reflexive Modernization: Politics, Tradition and Aesthetics in the Modern Social Order.* Cambridge: Polity Press.

Giddens, A. (1998). *The Third Way*, Polity: Cambridge, UK.

Gilbert T. (1998). Towards a Politics of Trust. *Journal of Advanced Nursing.* 27(6): p 1010-1016.

Gilbert T. (2005). Impersonal Trust and Professional Authority: Exploring the Dynamics. *Journal of Advanced Nursing,* 49(6): 568-577.

Gilbert T., Cochrane A. and Greenwell S. (2003). Professional discourse and service cultures: an organisational typology developed from health and welfare services for people with learning disabilities. *International Journal of Nursing Studies.* 40(7): 781 - 793.

Gilbert, T. (2001). Reflective Practice and Clinical Supervision: Meticulous rituals of the confessional, *Journal of Advanced Nursing* 36(2): 199 - 205.

Gilleard, C. and Higgs, P. (2001). *Cultures of Aging.* London: Prentice Hall.

Gilson, L. (2003). Trust and the development of health care a s a social institution. *Social Science and Medicine,* 56: 1453 – 1468.

Girrard, I. and Ogg, J. (1998). *Grand-parenting in France and England*, paper presented to the British Society of Gerontology, Sheffield, UK.

Gramsci, A. (1971). *Selections from the Prison Notebooks.* London: Lawrence and Wishart.

Gray, J. (1995). *Enlightenment's Wake*, Routledge: London.

Gruber, J, and Wise, DA, (eds.) (2004). *Social Security Programs and Retirement around the World. Micro Estimation.* Chicago, IL: University of Chicago Press.

Gruber, J, and Wise, DA, (eds.) (1999). *Social Security and Retirement around the World.* Chicago, IL: University of Chicago Press, 1999.

Guardian-ICM Poll. (2001). *Grandparenting and Retirement Activities*, ICM: London.

Gubrium, J.F. (1992). *Out of Control: Family Therapy and Domestic Disorder*, Sage: Thousand Oaks, CA.

Hardey M. (2005). Writing Digital Selves: Narratives of Health and Illness on the Internet, in M King and K Watson [eds.] *Representing Health:*

Discourses of health and Illness in the media. Basingstoke: Palgrave Macmillan pp 133 – 150.

Hardill, I. and Baines, S. and 6, P., (2007). Volunteering for all? Explaining patterns of volunteering and identifying strategies to promote it, *Policy and Politics.* 35 (3): 395-412.

Hargrave, T. and Anderson, W. (1992). *Finishing Well: Aging and Reparation in the Intergenerational Family*, Brunner and Mazel: New York.

Hayden, C., Boaz, A., and Taylor, F. (1999). Attitudes and Aspirations of Older People: A Qualitative Study, *DSS Research Report*, No. 102, CDS, London.

Help the Age International. (2000). *The Mark of a Noble Society.* London: Help Age International.

Hermalin, A., (ed.) (2002). *The Well-Being of the Elderly in Asia: A Four-Country Comparative Study.* Ann Arbor, MI: University of Michigan Press.

Holstein, J. and Gubrium, J. (2000). *The Self We Live By*, Oxford University Press: Oxford, UK.

Holtzman, R.A. (1997). *A World Bank Perspective on Pension Reform.* Paper prepared for the joint ILO-OECD Workshop on the Development and Reform of Pension Schemes, Paris, December.

International Monetary Fund. *The Economics of Demographics. Finance and Development. September* (2006);). 43(3). Available at: http://www.imf.org/external/pubs/ft/fandd/2006/09/.

Izuhara, M. (2000). *Family Change and Housing in Postwar Japanese Society*, Ashgate: Aldershot, UK.

James, J. (2005). Society: Frontline fighter: the social worker sacked for failing to prevent the murder of Victoria Climbie has won the right to resume working with children. *Guardian Society* 15th June pg 12.

Johnson, T. (2001). Governmentality and the institutionalization of expertise, in M Purdy and D Banks [eds.], *The Sociology and Politics of Health: A Reader*. London: Routledge pp 135-143.

Katz, S. (1996). *Disciplining old age: the formation of gerontological knowledge*, Charlottesville, VA: Virginia University Press.

Katz, S. (1999). Busy Bodies: Activity, Aging, and the Management of Everyday Life, *Journal of Aging Studies*, Vol. 14, No. 2, pp. 135-52.

Kemshall, H. (2002). *Risk, Social Policy and Welfare*. Buckingham: Open University Press.

Kennedy, G. (1990). College Students Expectations of Grandparent and Grandchild Role Behaviours, *The Gerontologist*, Vol. 30, No. 1, pp. 43-48.

Kenyon, G., Ruth, J., and Mader, W. (1999). Elements of a Narrative Gerontology, in V. Bengtson and K. Schaie (eds.), *Handbook of Theories of Ageing*, Springer: New York.

Kim, S., and Lee, J.-W., (2007). "Demographic changes, saving and current account in East Asia", *Asian Economic Papers*, 6(2).

Kinsella, K, and Velkoff, VA. (2001). *An Aging World: 2001*. Washington, DC: National Institute on Aging and U.S. Census Bureau.

Kivnick, H. (1988). Grandparenthood, Life Review and Psychosocial Development, *Journal of Gerontological Social Work*, Vol. 12, No. 3, pp. 63-82.

Krug, E. G. (2002). *World Report on Violence and Health*. Geneva: World Health Organisation.

Land, H. (1999). *The Changing Worlds of Work and Families*, Open University Press: Buckingham, UK.

Lane, C. (1998). Introduction: Theories and Issues in the Study of Trust, in C Lane & B Bachmann [eds.]. *Trust Within and Between Organisations: Conceptual issues and empirical applications.* Oxford: Oxford University Press pp 1 - 30.

Laville, S. (2005). 'Doctor justifies his role in baby death cases', *The Guardian,* Saturday July 2nd p. 6.

Le Grand, J. (2000). From Knight to Knave? Public Policy and Market Incentives, in P Taylor-Gooby [ed.] *Risk, Trust and Welfare*. Basingstoke: Macmillan pp 21 – 31.

Le Grand, J. (2003). *Motivation, Agency and Public Policy: Of Knights and Knaves, Prawns and Queens,* Oxford: Oxford University Press.

Lee-Treweek, G. (2002). Trust in Complementary Medicine: The case of cranial osteopathy, *The Sociological Review,* 50(1): 48 – 68.

Lewis, G. (2000). Introduction: Expanding the social policy imaginary, in Lewis, G., Gewirtz, S. and Clarke, J. (eds.). *Rethinking Social Policy.* London: Open University/Sage Publications.

Lewis, R., & Gillam, S. (2003). Back to the Market: Yet more reform to the National Health Service. *International journal of Health Services,* 33(1): 77 – 84.

Longino, C. F. (1994). 'Pressure from our aging population will broaden our understanding of medicine.' *Academic Medicine, 72* (10), 841-847.

Lopez, AD, Mathers, CD, Ezzati, M, Jamison, DT, and Murray, CJL, (eds.) (2006). *Global Burden of Disease and Risk Factors.* Washington, DC: The World Bank Group.

Luhmann N. (1979). *Trust and Power.* New York, NY: John Wiley and Sons.

Lunt, P., and Blundell, J. (2000). Public understanding of financial risk, in Taylor-Gooby, P. [ed.] *Risk, Trust and Welfare.* London: Macmillan pp 114 - 130.

Manton, KG and Gu, X. (2001). *Changes in the prevalence of chronic disability in the United States black and nonblack population above age 65 from 1982 to 1999.* Proceedings of the National Academy of Sciences 98;6354-6359.

May, T. and Powell, J.L. (2008). *Situating Social Theory 2.* McGraw Hill: Maidenhead.

McAdams, D. (1993). *The Stories We Live By*, Morrow: New York.

McIvor R, McHugh M, & Cadden C. (2002). Internet technologies: supporting transparency in the public sector. *International Journal of Public Sector Management,* 15(3): pp 170 – 187.

McLeod, J. (1997). *Narrative and Psychotherapy*, Sage: London.

Mechanic, D. (1998). Public trust and initiatives for new health care partnerships. *The Milbank Quarterly.* 76(2), 281-302.

Miller, T. (1993). *The Well-Tempered Self: Citizenship, Culture and the Postmodern Subject.* Baltimore: John Hopkins University Press.

Mills, T. (1999). When Grandchildren Grow Up, *Journal of Aging Studies,* Vol. 13, No. 2, pp. 219-39.

Minkler, M. (1999). Intergenerational Households Headed by Grandparents: Con-texts, Realities and Implications for Policy, *Journal of Aging Studies*, Vol. 13, No. 2, pp. 199-218.

Misztal, B, A. (1996). *Trust in Modern Societies*. Cambridge: Polity Press.

Möllering, G., (2001). The Nature of Trust: From Georg Simmel to a theory of Expectation, interpretation and suspension. *Sociology*, 35(2): 404 – 420.

Moody, H.R. (1998). *Aging, concepts and controversies*, Thousand Oaks: Pie Forge Press, Sage.

Murray, G. (1998). *China: the next superpower*, London: China Library.

Nanlan, Wu (2003). *China improves life for the elderly*. http://www.china.org.cn.htm accessed 23rd May 2006.

Newman, J. (1998). The Dynamics of Trust, in A, Coulson [ed.] *Trust and Contracts: Relationships in Local Government, Health and Public Services*. Bristol: Polity Press.

Organisation for Economic Cooperation and Development (OECD) Directorate for Employment, Labour and Social Affairs. (2007). *Disability Trends among Elderly People: Re-Assessing the Evidence in 12 OECD Countries* (Interim Report). Paris, France: OECD.

Osborne, T. (1997). Of Health and Statecraft. In Petersen A & Bunton R [eds.] *Foucault: Health and Medicine*. London: Routledge.

Pannell, C.W. (2002). 'China's continuing urban transition', *Environment and Planning A*, 34: 1571-1589.

Petersen, A. (1997). Risk, governance and the new public health, (Petersen A. & Bunton R. eds.) *Foucault: Health and Medicine*. London: Routledge, pp 189 – 206.

Phillipson, C. (1998). *Reconstructing Old Age*, Sage: London.

Phillipson, C., Bernard, M., Phillips, J., and Ogg, J. (2000). *The Family and Community Life of Older People*, Routledge: London.

Pillemer, K. and Wolf, R. (1986). *Elder Abuse: Conflict in the Family*, Auburn House: Westport, CT.

Powell, J.L. (2001). 'Theorizing gerontology: the case of old age, professional power and social policy in the United Kingdom', *Journal of Aging and Identity*, 6, 3: 117-135.

References

Powell, J.L. (2005) *Social Theory and Aging*. Rowman and Littlefield: Lanham.

Powell, J.L. (2014). *Social Gerontology*, Nova Science Publishers, Inc.: NY.

Powell, J.P. and Biggs, S. (2000). 'Managing old age: the disciplinary web of power, surveillance and normalisation', *Journal of Aging and Identity*, 5, 1: 3-13.

Powell, J. and Biggs, S. (2001). Rethinking Structure and Agency: Bio-Ethics, Aging and Technologies of the Self, *Sincronia*, Winter.

Powell, J.P. and Cook, I.G. (2000). 'A tiger behind and coming up fast: governmentality and the politics of population control in China', *Journal of Aging and Identity*, 5, 2: 79-89.

Powell, J.P. and Cook, I.G. (2001). 'Understanding Foucauldian gerontology: the Chinese state and the surveillance of older people', *International Journal of Society, Language and Culture*, 8, 1: 1-9.

Powell, J.P. and Cook, I.G. (2006). 'Unpacking patriarchy: a case study of patriarchy and the elderly in China' *International Journal of Sociology and Social Policy*, in press.

Powell, J. and Owen, T. (2007). *Reconstructing Postmodernism: Critical Debates*, Nova Science Publishers, Inc.: New York.

Powell, J.L. (2005). *Social Theory and Aging*, Rowman and Littlefield: NY.

Price, D., and Ginn, J. (2003). Sharing the crust? Gender, partnership status and inequalities in pension accumulation, in Arber, S., Davidson, K., and Ginn, J. [eds.] *Gender and Ageing: changing roles and relationships*. Buckingham: Open University Press 127 - 147.

Putnam, R. D. (1993). *Making Democracy Work: Civic traditions in modern Italy*. Princetown: Princetown University Press.

Qualls, S. (1999). Realising Power in Intergenerational Hierachies, in M. Duffy (ed.), *Handbook of Counselling and Psychotherapy with Older Adults*, Wiley: New York.

Roberto, K. (1990). Grandparent and Grand-child Relationships, in T.H. Brubaker (ed.), *Family Relationships in Later Life*, Sage: London.

Rose, N. (1993). 'Government, Authority, and Expertise in Advanced Liberalism'*, Economy and Society*, 22, (3): 283-99.

Rose, N. (1996). The death of the social? Re-figuring the territory of government. *Economy and Society*. 25(3), 327-356.

Rose, N. (1999). *Powers of Freedom: Reframing political thought*. Cambridge: Cambridge University Press.

Rose, N. and Miller, P. (1992). 'Political Power Beyond the State: Problematics of Government', *The British Journal of Sociology*, 43, (2), 172-205.

Rothstein, B. (2000). Trust, Social Dilemmas and Collective Memories, *Journal of Theoretical Politics*, 12(4): 477 – 501.

Ryff, C. and Seltzer, M. (1996). *The Parental Experience in Midlife*, Chicago University Press: Chicago, IL.

Scharf, T. and Wenger, G. (1995)., *International Perspectives on Community Care for Older People*, Avebury: Al-dershot, UK.

Schreck, H. (2000). *Community and Caring*, UPA: New York.

Seligman, A. B. (1997). *The Problem of Trust*. Princetown: Princetown University Press.

Shapiro, S. P. (1987). The social control of impersonal trust. *American Journal of Sociology*. November. 93(3): pp 623-658.

Shaw, S. (2001). External Assessment of Health Care. *British Medical Journal,* 322(7290): 851 – 854.

Silverstein, M. and Bengtson, V.L. (1997). Intergenerational Solidarity and the Structure of Adult Child-Parent Relationships in American Families, *American Journal of Sociology*, Vol. 103, No. 2, pp. 429-60.

Stewart, D. and Wisniewski, M. (2004). Performance Measurement for stakeholders: The case of Scottish Local Authorities, *International Journal of Public Sector Management,* 17(2&3): pp 222 - 233.

Sztompka, P. (1999). *Trust: A Sociological Theory.* Cambridge: Cambridge University Press.

Taylor-Gooby P. (1999). Markets and Motives: Trust and Egoism in Welfare Markets. *Journal of Social Policy*, 28(1): 97 – 114.

Taylor-Gooby P. (2000). Risk and Welfare, in P Taylor-Gooby [ed.] *Risk, Trust and Welfare*. Basingstoke: Macmillan pp 1 – 20.

Thompson, P. (1999). The Role of Grandparents When Parents Part or Die: Some Reflections on the Mythical Decline of the Extended Family, *Ageing and Society*, Vol. 19, No. 4, pp. 471-503.

Thomson, E. and Minkler, M. (2001). American Grandparents Providing Extensive Childcare to Their Grand-children: Prevalence and Profile, *The Gerontologist*, Vol. 41, No. 2, pp. 201-09.

Tulloch, J. and Lupton, D. (2003). *Risk and Everyday Life*. London: Sage.

UKG, UK Government. (1981). *Growing Older*, HMSO: London.

UKG, UK Government. (1989). *Community Care: An Agenda for Action*, HMSO: London.

UKG, UK Government. (1990). *NHS and Community Care Act*, HMSO: London.

UKG, UK Government. (1993). *No Longer Afraid: The Safeguard of Older People in Domestic Settings*, HMSO: London.

UKG, UK Government. (2000a). *Winning the Generation Game*, www.cabinet-office.gov.uk.

UKG, UK Government. (2000b). *Supporting Families*, HMSO: London.

United Nations Department of Economic and Social Affair (2002). *Population Division. World Population Ageing 1950–2050*. New York: United Nations.

Uslaner, E. M. (1999). Democracy and Social Capital, in M Warren [ed.]. *Democracy and Trust*. Cambridge: Cambridge University Press pp 121 - 150.

Waldrop, D., Weber, J., Herald, S., Pruett, J., Cooper, K., and Jouzapavicius, K. (1999). Wisdom and Life Experience: How Grandfathers Mentor Their Grandchildren, *Journal of Aging and Identity*, Vol. 4, No. 1, pp. 33-46.

Walker, A. and Aspalter, C. (eds.) (2008). *Securing the Future for Old Age in Europe*, Casa Verde: Hong Kong.

Walker, A. and Naegele, G. (1999). *The Politics of Old Age in Europe*, Open University Press: Buckingham, UK.

Walker, A. and Naeghele, G. (2000). *The Politics of Ageing in Europe*. OUP: Milton Keynes.

Walker, Alan. (2002). A Strategy for Active Ageing, *International Social Security Review*, Vol. 55, No. 1, pp. 121-39.

Watson, S. (2000). Foucault and the study of social policy, in Lewis, G., Gewirtz, S. and Clarke, J. (eds.). *Rethinking Social Policy.* London: Open University/Sage Publications.

Welsh, T., and Pringle, M. (2001). Editorial. Social Capital: Trusts need to recreate trust. *British Medical Journal,* 323: 177 – 178.

Wenger, C. (1984). *Support Networks for Older People*, CSPRD: Bangor, UK.

Williamson, J.B. and Deitelbaum, C. (2005). 'Social security reform: does partial privatisation make sense for China?', *Journal of Aging Studies*, 19: 257-271.

Wu, F. (ed.) (2006). *Globalisation and the Chinese City*, London: Routledge.

Wu Nanlan (2003) 'China improves life for the elderly', http://www.china.org.cn.htm accessed 23rd May 2006.

Zhang Benbo, Zhang (2002). *'Ageing population requires new action'*, China Population Information Research Centre, http://www.cpirc.org.cn/en/enews20020329.htm, accessed 17th October 2005.

Author's Contact Information

Professor Jason L. Powell
PhD, FHEA, FRSPH, FRSA
Professor of Social Gerontology and Sociology
Department of Social and Political Science
The University of Chester,
Chester, UK
jasonpwll3@gmail.com

INDEX

A

accountability, 40, 52, 55, 58, 69, 105
adults, 21, 52, 53, 86, 88, 91, 93, 94, 97
Africa, 13, 18, 19, 20, 103
age, 4, 5, 6, 7, 8, 10, 11, 12, 13, 14, 15, 16, 17, 18, 19, 21, 23, 24, 25, 27, 28, 29, 30, 85, 89, 90, 92, 93, 99, 104
aging population, 78, 101
agencies, 34, 39, 40, 57, 81, 89, 92
aging identity, 30, 98, 99
aging population, 7, 9, 10, 11, 13, 17, 25, 26, 86, 104
aging process, 4, 5
aging society, 29
aging studies, 23
analytical framework, 37
articulation, 62, 73, 78, 80
asylum, 63, 65
attitudes, 2, 3, 7, 28
audit, 53, 56, 57, 58, 72, 74
autonomy, 35, 40, 55, 56, 58, 78, 80, 88

B

banking, 16
behaviors, 2, 94
benefits, 14, 26, 62, 69, 72, 83
benign, 62, 76, 83
birth rate, 9, 11
births, 10
blame, 58, 61
blood, 4
bonds, 68, 73
breakdown, 5, 6, 94
Britain, 88, 89, 107
budget deficit, 14
bureaucratization, 42

C

capitalism, 24, 28
cardiovascular function, 4
caregivers, 96
charities, 51, 89
chemical, 6
Chicago, 104, 110

Index

child abuse, 58, 63
child mortality, 19
child protection, 58
childcare, 93, 95
childhood, 70
children, 9, 12, 17, 18, 19, 21, 52, 53, 93, 94, 95, 96, 101, 110, 111
China, iii, 10, 17, 20, 21, 101, 102, 103, 105
citizens, 46, 87, 88, 89
citizenship, 10, 46, 76, 77, 85, 107
civic life, 18
civil servants, 14, 21
civil society, 88
civilization, 34
clients, 35, 40, 42, 47, 48, 55, 56, 58, 59, 60, 61, 65, 71
cognitive capacities, 1
coherence, 50, 68, 77, 97
colonisation, 78, 81
commodity, 75, 78, 83, 105
communication, 53, 56, 57, 60, 64, 70, 88, 95
communication skills, 70
communication technologies, 53, 56, 60, 64
communitarianism, 88
community relations, 71
competition, 40, 52, 77, 91
complexity, 28, 61, 64, 72, 74
conception, 40, 58
conceptualization, 30, 68, 82
conflict, 27, 50, 75, 82, 93, 100
consensus, 27, 45
consolidation, 25, 33, 82, 85
construction, 29, 34, 45, 84, 91
consumer sovereignty, 36
consumers, 37, 39, 79, 90
consumption, 93
cost, 14, 58, 69
cost effectiveness, 14
counterbalance, 55
covering, 16, 52
critical analysis, 45

criticism, 63
culture, 3, 7, 24, 32, 39, 58, 68
currency, 14
current account, 104
customers, 40, 81

D

dance, 49, 50, 55, 60
danger, 33, 80
deaths, 5, 10, 63
decay, 7, 24, 34
deinstitutionalization, 36
democracy, 91, 94, 96
demographic change, 10, 25, 91
demographic transition, 9
developed countries, 10, 11, 16
developed nations, 9
developing countries, 9, 12, 14, 19
disability, 18, 25, 29, 104
discrimination, 29, 58
diseases, 3, 5, 6
distribution, 25, 27, 28, 49, 59
diversity, 30, 39
dominance, 7, 78
drug abuse, 96

E

East Asia, 20, 104
economic change, 19
economic institutions, 43
economic power, 24
economic transformation, 30
education, 10, 20, 52, 79
elderly population, 33
elders, 87, 89, 92
emerging markets, 17
employment, 10, 29, 68, 82, 90
employment status, 10
empowerment, 35, 38, 63, 65, 77

England, 29, 52, 57, 106, 108
entrepreneurs, 38, 76
entrepreneurship, 88
ethics, 65, 105, 107
ethnic groups, 96
ethnicity, 10, 28
Europe, 9, 10, 13, 15, 16, 17, 20, 85, 88, 105, 110, 114
everyday life, 71, 84
evidence, 6, 17, 29, 41, 51, 59, 60, 74, 80, 87, 95
exclusion, 25, 85, 99
exercise, 29, 36, 38, 39, 47, 50, 51, 55, 56, 60, 64, 69, 75, 76
expert systems, 34
expertise, 34, 38, 40, 52, 55, 61, 69, 71, 73, 74, 75, 78, 79, 80, 81, 82, 112

F

face-to-face interaction, 47
faith, 34, 68, 72
families, 9, 10, 11, 19, 20, 21, 52, 53, 58, 69, 83, 84, 86, 87, 88, 89, 91, 92, 94, 96, 97, 99, 100
family life, 84, 85, 86, 88, 90, 97
family members, 98
family support, 21, 58
family system, 94
family therapy, 93
fear, 17, 20
fertility, 9, 10, 12, 19, 20
fertility rate, 12, 20
financial, 15, 16, 19, 42, 88, 94, 112
financial markets, 15
financial support, 94
Foucault, Michel, ii, iii
France, 16, 90, 105, 108

G

Germany, 16, 17, 88, 90, 95
gerontology, 1, 2, 3, 7, 23, 24, 26, 27, 29, 30, 32, 102, 103
global aging, 11
globalization, 88
goods and services, 39
governance, 37, 39, 64, 78, 113
government intervention, 26
governments, 12, 15, 17, 24, 35, 46, 68, 83, 85
governor, 54
gross domestic product, 16
growth, 13, 24, 89, 90, 98

H

hair, 4, 7
hair loss, 4, 7
health, 7, 10, 11, 13, 18, 20, 26, 40, 48, 52, 55, 56, 59, 69, 71, 72, 73, 75, 76, 77, 78, 79, 80, 81, 82, 83, 101, 102, 111, 112
health care, 10, 20, 72, 81, 101, 111, 112
health services, 72, 75
hegemony, 81, 98
historical overview, 23
history, 3, 12, 17, 24, 25, 32, 91, 94, 97, 105
human, 3, 4, 6, 8, 11, 20, 32, 33, 42, 47, 68, 70, 71, 82, 83
human activity, 83
human body, 3, 6
human condition, 3
human organisms, 4
human right, 11, 20
human sciences, 47
human subjects, 47

I

identity, 8, 23, 25, 30, 33, 35, 43, 47, 48, 49, 51, 62, 65, 68, 76, 84, 94, 97, 98, 100
images, 24, 40
Independence, 52, 77, 80, 106
individual character, 10
individual characteristics, 10
individualism, 86
individualization, 34
individuals, 2, 5, 6, 12, 13, 27, 32, 34, 35, 36, 39, 43, 46, 48, 49, 50, 51, 52, 62, 63, 68, 70, 72, 73, 74, 75, 76, 77, 81, 82, 83, 84, 85
industrialized countries, 20
inequality, 27, 96
infrastructure, 16, 59
insertion, 39, 59
inspections, 72
institutions, 3, 26, 33, 36, 38, 39, 46, 47, 67, 68, 69, 73, 78, 79, 80
intellectual disabilities, 58
interference, 85
international trade, 16
interpersonal relations, 84
interpersonal relationships, 84
intervention, 23, 37, 78
issues, 11, 13, 20, 23, 27, 29, 39, 55, 56, 68, 72, 82, 85, 86, 96, 112

J

Japan, 11, 20, 95
journalists, 63
jurisdiction, 80, 81

K

Keynes, 101, 103, 105
kinship network, 18

L

labor force, 93
landscape, 26, 64, 75, 80, 97
later life, 8, 11, 14, 18, 19, 97, 98, 99
learning disabilities, 111
life course, 1, 8, 21, 30, 43, 45, 83
life expectancy, 9, 11, 12, 13, 19
living arrangements, 13
living conditions, 18
local community, 82
local government, 77
love, 68, 95

M

mandatory retirement, 3
marginalization, 28
marriage, 10, 79
media, 9, 63, 111
medical, 1, 2, 3, 6, 7, 8, 21, 31, 32, 48, 72, 81, 102
medicine, 2, 3, 9, 33, 48, 54, 81, 104
mental health, 59, 63
mentor, 91, 92
mentoring, 90, 92
metaphor, 41
methodology, 31, 32
mixed economy, 36, 37
modern society, 7, 59, 69
modernity, 23, 33, 67, 73, 76
moral imperative, 46
mortality, 9, 10
multinational companies, 16
murder, 111
mutual respect, 88

N

narratives, 2, 7, 23, 30, 32, 43, 47, 84, 85, 86, 88, 90, 91, 92, 94, 96, 97, 98, 99, 100
nation states, 10, 12, 16
national identity, 68
national strategy, 106
nationality, 10
natural disaster, 86
negative consequences, 28, 58
negotiation, 61, 84, 87, 96
neoliberalism, 36, 39, 85, 96
North America, 9, 13, 14, 45, 88

O

old age, 2, 4, 6, 8, 17, 23, 24, 25, 27, 28, 29, 30, 31, 32, 34, 35, 43, 47, 48, 85, 93, 96, 101, 102
opportunities, 53, 75, 89
oppression, 65
osteopathy, 81, 112

P

parenting, 85, 90, 91, 92, 93, 94, 95, 96, 108
parents, 58, 82, 90, 94, 95
pension plans, 15
per capita income, 19
performance indicator, 58, 62
personal identity, 84
personal relations, 26
personal relationship, 26
personal responsibility, 63
policy, 18, 20, 23, 24, 25, 26, 28, 35, 36, 37, 39, 41, 43, 46, 48, 52, 53, 54, 57, 58, 59, 61, 76, 77, 80, 81, 82, 83, 84, 85, 86, 87, 88, 89, 90, 91, 92, 93, 94, 95, 96, 97, 99, 102
policy initiative, 77, 86, 89

policy makers, 24, 57
political affiliations, 52
political parties, 17, 35
political power, 54
politics, 49, 52, 53, 57, 60, 61, 64, 83, 88, 102
pollution, 5
population, 9, 11, 12, 13, 14, 15, 16, 17, 18, 19, 20, 21, 38, 46, 50, 52, 69, 72, 73, 75, 80, 81, 83, 90, 96, 102, 103, 104
population control, 102
population size, 10
population structure, 16
positive aging, 92
positive correlation, 71
postural hypotension, 5
poverty, 14, 18, 20, 28, 29
power relations, 27, 32, 46, 48, 50, 53, 54, 59, 61, 65
pressure groups, 89
primacy, 39, 81
private sector, 42, 57, 77
privatization, 20, 37, 39
professional development, 64
professionalism, 43, 54, 55
professionalization, 38
professionals, 7, 40, 47, 48, 49, 50, 51, 52, 54, 55, 56, 57, 60, 61, 63, 67, 69, 70, 73, 75, 78, 79, 80, 81, 82, 83, 86, 92, 99
project, 28, 33, 46, 47, 65, 87, 91
psychoanalysis, 34
public domain, 86
public finance, 17
public health, 9, 12, 63, 77, 113
public interest, 15
public pension, 14, 15
public policy, 86
public sector, 16, 36, 39, 56, 112
public service, 16, 36, 91
public welfare, 34

R

race, 10, 25, 28, 29, 96
reciprocity, 72, 93
resistance, 50, 54, 56, 57, 60, 62, 63, 65, 79
resources, 27, 28, 29, 35, 41, 43, 61, 99
retirement, 14, 15, 17, 20, 28
retirement age, 14, 17, 20
rhetoric, 57, 84, 92, 97

S

school, 26, 33, 40, 46, 52, 64, 90, 91
science, 2, 33, 56, 67
scientific knowledge, 73
security, 18, 38, 68, 70, 91, 103
self-discipline, 55
self-interest, 79
self-knowledge, 48, 51
self-regulation, 52, 79
self-report data, 95
service provider, 90
social capital, 68, 71, 72, 74, 79
social care, 39, 42, 52, 53, 56, 69, 70, 71, 72, 73, 76, 80, 81, 82, 83
social change, 13, 69, 78
social construct, 2, 37, 43
social context, 43, 50, 52, 76
social control, 2, 33, 79, 114
social environment, 2, 68
social exclusion, 20, 96
social fabric, 75, 78, 82, 87
social gerontology, 23, 24, 26, 31
social group, 38, 91
social infrastructure, 16
social institutions, 51, 52, 78
social interaction, 76
social life, 28, 39, 50, 67
social network, 14, 50, 95
social order, 33, 68
social policy, 23, 24, 25, 26, 31, 35, 39, 49, 51, 59, 65, 81, 83, 84, 88, 96, 97, 99, 102, 112, 114
social problems, 24, 27, 28, 30, 33, 77
social relations, 26, 32, 35, 40, 43, 50, 68, 70, 81, 85
social relationships, 26, 32, 35, 40, 50, 68, 70, 81
social sciences, 33, 67, 82, 84
social theory, 25, 67
social welfare, 7, 36, 40, 45, 47, 48, 55, 57, 81, 101
social withdrawal, 2
social work practitioners, 55
social workers, 7, 31, 33, 34, 35, 46, 47, 48, 49, 53, 55, 56, 58, 60, 61, 63, 64, 65
society, 1, 2, 3, 8, 12, 23, 26, 27, 28, 29, 34, 39, 49, 62, 63, 69, 74, 78, 88, 90, 91, 111
sociology, 25, 42, 43
solidarity, 85, 87, 93
sovereign state, 15
specialisation, 53
specific knowledge, 51
state control, 40
state intervention, 75, 77
stress, 40, 91, 94
subjective experience, 30
subjectivity, 8, 27, 30, 47, 50, 54, 65
supervision, 54, 56, 60, 64
surveillance, 32, 33, 34, 46, 50, 51, 53, 55, 56, 57, 58, 59, 60, 64, 78, 80, 81, 85, 86, 97, 102, 103
survival, 4, 5, 17, 74

T

tactics, 38, 54, 58, 59, 60, 69, 74, 79
techniques, 3, 31, 32, 38, 47, 49, 51, 63, 64, 72, 75, 79, 80
technologies, 38, 40, 41, 42, 47, 48, 49, 51, 55, 56, 57, 59, 64, 65, 75, 76, 112

theoretical approach, 28
theoretical assumptions, 6
trade union, 52
traditions, 8, 34, 113
training, 53, 54
transmission, 94
transparency, 68, 71, 79, 112
treatment, 2, 28, 30, 34, 81
trustworthiness, 71, 72, 73, 75, 76

U

United Kingdom, vii, 23, 24, 26, 27, 28, 29, 31, 35, 36, 37, 42, 45, 102
United Nations, 105
United States, 10, 13, 14, 26, 27, 31, 59, 72, 90, 94, 104
universities, 46
urban, 9, 102

V

vaccine, 73
vein, 28, 58, 59
victims, 91
violence, 88

W

war, 17, 26, 45
war years, 26
wealth, 14, 18, 20
web, 51, 64, 79, 102
welfare, iii, 16, 18, 27, 28, 34, 36, 37, 39, 40, 41, 42, 45, 47, 48, 53, 54, 55, 58, 65, 77, 78, 79, 81, 86, 87, 111
welfare state, 16, 34, 39, 41
welfare system, 48, 55
well-being, 27, 46, 52
withdrawal, 26, 27, 92
work activity, 55, 58, 62, 64, 65
work roles, 26
workers, 10, 14, 16, 17, 20, 21, 26, 42, 53, 56, 58, 62, 63, 65, 90
workforce, 16, 20
working conditions, 4
working population, 90
worldwide, 12, 20

Y

young people, 17, 18, 89